CONDEMNED
FOR LOVE
in
OLD VIRGINIA

CONDEMNED FOR LOVE

in

OLD VIRGINIA

The Lynching of Arthur Jordan

JIM HALL

INTRODUCTION BY CLAUDINE L. FERRELL, PHD

THE
History
PRESS

Published by The History Press
Charleston, SC
www.historypress.com

Front cover silhouettes: Courtesy of Lucy Elliott.

First published 2023

Manufactured in the United States

ISBN 9781467154598

Library of Congress Control Number: 2023932151

CONTENTS

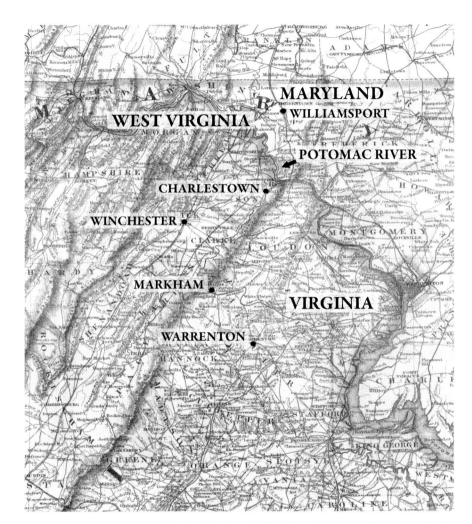

This 1876 map shows some of the key locations in Virginia and Maryland in the travels of Arthur Jordan and Elvira Corder. *Library of Congress.*

PREFACE

I met Kirk Goolsby in 2018 after he emailed me about Arthur Jordan's death. I knew about the Jordan case—an 1880 Fauquier County, Virginia lynching—but it was Goolsby who encouraged me to look closer at it. His interest inspired mine, and the result is this book.

Goolsby is a teacher at Northern Virginia Community College, a big, friendly man with a handlebar mustache. His passion for history once drove him to find and interview as many World War I veterans as he could. More recently, he and his wife, Robin, bought Brentmoor, once a museum dedicated to Confederate colonel John S. Mosby on Main Street in downtown Warrenton, Virginia. They renovated the building, and it is now the family home.

In his email, Goolsby said that Jordan's death "is not well known nor well publicized here." I now know that to be true. Once, when I wrote to ask the help of a prominent Fauquier historian, she replied that she had never heard of Jordan. She asked to see evidence of his lynching, and she added that perhaps I was confusing Warrenton, Virginia, with one of the other Warrentons that existed in the United States in 1880. I sent her newspaper accounts and a copy of the inquiry done by the county coroner. To her credit, she replied, that, yes, I had found a lynching that was not widely known.

Goolsby, on the other hand, knew a lot about Jordan's death. He walked through the Warrenton Cemetery one time, looking for an old locust tree, the type reported to be Jordan's hanging tree. No luck. Then he searched online and found a sketch done the morning after the hanging by Dr. Gustavus R.B. Horner, a local physician. The drawing is now part of the Horner collection at the University of Virginia library. When Horner learned of the lynching, he went to the cemetery to find Jordan's corpse still suspended.

Horner's drawing shows a boundary fence with a stile, or steps, in the foreground. At mid-scene, Jordan hangs with his hands tied behind him and a wooden bit tied around his neck, the stick that was originally placed in his mouth by his killers to silence him. More importantly, the sketch includes other landmarks within the cemetery.

One of those landmarks is the Confederate Memorial, a marble spire built in 1877 that marks the burial place of hundreds of Confederate soldiers. Horner appears to have added the memorial to his drawing as an afterthought. By placing it to the left of the suspended body, he provided Goolsby with a powerful clue.

Goolsby set out from his home again, sweeping through the cemetery near the memorial. "I knew I was in the right area," he said. "Then, I distinctly remember turning to see where the tree would have been, expecting it to be a void of grass and newer gravestones. But there was a tree, a massive ash tree. It was standing right where the sketch said it should be."

Goolsby was not troubled that his discovery was an ash tree and not a locust. "Both tree species have similar, pinnately compound leaves," said the biology teacher. Besides, the reporters who wrote the stories relied on others to tell them what happened. None of them was present at the hanging.

Kirk Goolsby in the Warrenton Cemetery at the site of Arthur Jordan's hanging. Goolsby holds the Horner drawing of the hanging. *Author's collection.*

Goolsby was also encouraged by what seemed to be a puzzling feature of Horner's sketch. The physician placed a single tombstone in his drawing, located on a line between Jordan's body and the monument. Today, the Warrenton Cemetery is one of the largest in the region, covering a dozen blocks downtown and containing more than eight thousand graves. Why had Horner included only one tombstone in his drawing? Surely there were dozens of others he could have included. But after walking the grounds, Goolsby discovered that Horner faithfully sketched what he saw. Only one of the present-day stones, marking the death of James Deshields, dates to before 1880, and its shape matches the one depicted in Horner's drawing.

"I do think I have located the spot, and even more stunning, I believe I may have discovered the exact tree that was used," he concluded.

He invited me to meet him at the cemetery. Indeed, when I saw him stand on the spot, drawing in hand, and point uphill to the Confederate Memorial, I was convinced he had found the place where the mob killed Jordan. More than 140 years had passed since the murder, and dozens of graves had been dug on the hillside—yet the location was still recognizable.

But Goolsby was troubled. The suspected tree was plagued by the emerald ash borer, a destructive beetle. Many of its limbs were bare though they should have been dressed in a spring leaf cover. "The tree is not healthy," he said. "It is dying."

Goolsby predicted that the town, which owns the cemetery, would remove the tree. He was correct. One year later, a maintenance crew swept through the cemetery, clearing all damaged and diseased trees. The tree was gone.

Later, one of the cemetery workers told me that the tree crew was so impressed with the giant tree that they counted the rings to see how old it was. He apologized that their count was not as good as it could have been—they counted the rings in only one section of the trunk and multiplied by the estimated number of sections. Their tally was 140 years, a number that didn't confirm the tree's possible role in the hanging but didn't eliminate it either.

However, elimination came later, thanks to a diary entry Horner made at the time. Goolsby had found the location of the lynching but not the hanging tree. The ash he spotted was apparently a successor tree, perhaps growing from the original stump. The hanging tree was gone, cut down on the day after the murder.

The tree was an "unwitting participant" in Jordan's death, Goolsby said. Its loss makes it easier to forget what happened there. Perhaps a cenotaph, or stone marker, could replace it. The cenotaph would remind visitors that this is a place of burial, of eternal rest, but that it was also the site of a lynching. A hate-driven white mob killed a man there, a Black man whose only crime was that he and a white woman had fallen in love.

ACKNOWLEDGEMENTS

Once, during a talk to a community group in Berryville, Virginia, an audience member challenged one of the assumptions I made in my book *The Last Lynching in Northern Virginia*. I wrote that the corpse of a man found hanging from an apple tree on Rattlesnake Mountain in Fauquier County, Virginia, was Shedrick Thompson.

"How do you know that for sure?" the man asked.

I answered that Thompson's alleged crimes of assault and rape, his disappearance and the massive, two-month manhunt that followed were well publicized in the rural community. It made sense that when a farmhand checking his fence line found the decomposed body hanging in the mountain forest, he correctly identified it as the fugitive.

"How many other Black men would be hanging there?" I asked the man. But he was not convinced.

"Well, sir," I replied. "Why don't you write your own book on the Thompson case and say what you want? This is my version of what happened."

I thought of that man while working on this book, the story of Arthur Jordan and Elvira Corder. I spent many months learning about their interracial love affair, reading countless records, interviewing descendants and visiting the places where events happened. I labored without the kind of primary sources—letters, diaries, photos or family narratives—that researchers usually rely on.

As historian Martha Hodes said about cases such as this one, "A sexual liaison between a white woman and a black man was unlikely to be documented in any detail. Hardly anyone wrote about such liaisons in letters, or even in diaries, at least not in any detail and never in the first person."

Because of that, I had to write my way through the silence, using what Hodes describes as "the language of speculation." Words such as "perhaps" and "possibly" are sprinkled throughout this text. I was humbled by how hard it was to reconstruct events from more than 140 years ago, how I had to make informed guesses from scant clues. Still, I am proud of what I have accomplished. I bear witness here to a case of racial terror, an unpunished murder. This is my version of what happened to Arthur and Elvira. It is as true as I can make it.

Even so, Elvira's story is incomplete. I know that she was the oldest child in a successful farm family, that she made the fateful decision to love a Black man and that her family insisted that the choice was not hers to make. I also know that she lived under a violent intolerance, within both her home and community, and that that intolerance led to the lynching of Arthur Jordan.

Yet Elvira all but disappears from the public record after her flight with Arthur to Maryland. At first, this gap in the narrative—her silence—bothered me. I had many moments of doubt and considered setting aside the project. But I came to believe that the mystery of Elvira's fate is as interesting as established fact. As the artist Pieter Bruegel said, "Every story has its point of weakness. If it did not, there would be no need to tell the story. Straight life would suffice."

Despite the gap, this book illustrates one of the darkest chapters in America's long history of racial intolerance and violence. It is a tale of temptation and loss, of love pursued in a time of hate, of concealment and disastrous disclosure. It raises questions about family, honor and law in post-Reconstruction Virginia. It describes a conflict between genders and generations and illustrates the casual dehumanization of the other. Most importantly, it highlights the practice of lynching and the evil of racism, issues that are still with us.

I was lucky to have the support of many people while working on this project, all of whom shared my desire to illuminate a little-known event in Virginia history. The Sheffields, Art and Martha, offered valuable insights, as did Daryl Lease, a former newspaper colleague. Shawn Nicholls of Fauquier County, Virginia, was an early supporter of the project and provided many hours of important research. Sue Stone and Marsha Fuller, professional genealogists, tackled the Elvira question. Wendy Wheatcraft, preservation planner for Fauquier County, is so knowledgeable about local history that a one-hour appointment with her can quickly grow into two.

ACKNOWLEDGEMENTS

Dr. Claudine Ferrell, chair of the history department, and Jack Bales, librarian emeritus, both at the University of Mary Washington, must have wondered if I ever talked of anything other than finding Elvira. Yet they never discouraged me. Dr. Gianluca De Fazio, an associate professor at James Madison University and creator of the must-see Racial Terror: Lynching in Virginia website, read an early version of this manuscript and offered many helpful suggestions. Kirk Goolsby was an inspiration from the beginning of the project to the end.

I also benefited from the work of Alan Moll, who documented the descendants of Arthur Jordan, and David Corder, family historian for the Corders. My brothers, Thom Hall and Bernie Hall, helped with the research. And the Inkubators—a local writing group—encouraged me to keep writing, especially when I had doubts. They had no doubt that the fragments they were reading each month would someday become this book.

Librarians from my hometown of Fredericksburg, Virginia, at the Central Rappahannock Regional Library, were consistently helpful, as were employees at the Library of Virginia, the University of Mary Washington's Simpson Library, the Fauquier County Public Library, the Fauquier Heritage and Preservation Foundation, the Fauquier History Museum at the Old Jail, the Rappahannock Historical Society, the Washington County (Maryland) Free Library, the Thomas Balch Library, the Afro-American Historical Association of Fauquier County, the Virginia Historical Society and the Albert and Shirley Small Special Collections Library at the University of Virginia.

Finally, I am lucky (in many ways) to be married to Laura Moyer, a professional editor. People still call Laura the "Red Pen Lady," remembering a popular grammar column she wrote years ago for the *Fredericksburg Free Lance-Star* newspaper. With that red pen in hand, she read and reread this manuscript, recommending often painful changes. I made those changes, and the book is so much better because of them and her.

15

INTRODUCTION

A common definition of lynching is the killing of someone by three or more people for an alleged crime or violation of a social norm. Most such mob murders that have been recorded and studied were hangings, but others were shootings, burnings at the stake, beatings, drownings—in other words, any way that a life could be taken, especially if the means (and the public display) sent the appropriate message. That message for thousands of African Americans was about the racial order that whites had defined and were determined to protect. As Jim Hall makes clear through the story of Arthur Jordan, the messages were sometimes sent by families who saw their honor and their worldview threatened.

Some states enacted laws against lynching, but rulings of "death by persons unknown" and the public's support for how to handle African Americans who strayed from their assigned "place" prompted Congress to act at the turn of the twentieth century. But Congress's weak efforts to pass a federal law against lynching failed time after time in the first decades of the 1900s. So, (unenforced) state laws and (unenforced) national civil rights statutes continued to do little to halt the brutal uncertainty of life for African Americans. Beyond daily disrespect, beyond debt peonage, beyond voting denial and segregation, beyond limits on education and jobs and beyond white anger manifested in riots was, as in Arthur Jordan's time, the possibility of a white mob that decided that a Black man's behavior required the end of his life, often as painfully and mockingly and publicly as possible.

Jim Hall's first study of a Virginia lynching looked at the mob killing of Shedrick Thompson in the early 1930s when lynching as an accepted southern tool was beginning to see hope of an end. If nothing else, mob killings sent a message that the South (the location of most mob murders) was not "modern" and not a safe place for northern investment. His latest delving into the commonwealth's history takes him back to both a different and a similar time.

The end of the Civil War left Virginia with physical and emotional scars and with fears about how lives and livelihoods could continue without slave labor and without the controls and assurances that slavery provided for whites fearful of losing their social, economic and political status to an "inferior" race. Honor, safety and control were at stake. One solution was what African American newspapers would soon call "a national disgrace," "America's plague," "America's shame" and even "the national sin."

The story of Arthur Jordan and Elvira Corder is the story of a man and woman seeking a life together in postwar Virginia. The amended national constitution and related enforcement statutes—however blunted by Supreme Court decisions and new state constitutions and officials—offered a life hardly imagined only a few years earlier. Their hopes for the future, however, confronted others' determination to maintain the past. Elvira's family sought to protect themselves and their world, if not her.

When a cry of shame is uttered,
That a Negro has disgraced
The virtue of a maiden fair—
Mobs slaughter in our race…
I. Gustavus R. Ford, *Washington Bee*, April 8, 1916

Arthur and Elvira's story was, as this poem suggests, not unique. African American newspapers in the late 1800s and early 1900s presented similar tales, but Hall's look into the roots of this couple's shattered love and hopes provides a story of not only two young people and a family but also a state (and ultimately a country) struggling with and against its past, present and future.

Claudine L. Ferrell is a professor of history at the University of Mary Washington in Fredericksburg, Virginia. She has taught there since 1984. She holds a PhD from Rice University, where her doctoral research focused on lynching in the South. She is also the author of *Reconstruction* (2003) and *The Abolitionist Movement* (2005).

1

WE WANT JORDAN

The rumble of horses woke the dog first, and the dog woke Charles Martin. From his bedroom window, Martin looked down on Waterloo Turnpike near the old toll gate to see a parade of horsemen, dozens of them, entering the town of Warrenton, Virginia, from the west. Several had already passed beneath him. They must be on a cattle drive, he thought. Martin, a fifty-year-old cobbler, thought nothing more about it and went back to bed.

But the horsemen had other plans that night. They were headed for the Fauquier County Courthouse and Old Fauquier County Jail, a few blocks away in the center of town on the highest hill. They drew rein short of their destination. It was just before 2:00 a.m. on Monday, January 19, 1880. It was warm for a winter's night, and the quarter moon shed little light on the men's arrival. With masks pulled over their faces, they hoped no one would recognize them.

The riders dismounted and divided into two groups. One group stayed with the horses. The other blackened the face of one of their own, tied his hands in front and placed a "guard" at each shoulder. At the jail, several crouched in the shadows while the others pounded on the jail door.

Jailer Horace Pattie woke and went to his bedroom window upstairs.

"Who's there?" he called.

"A prisoner from Rectortown," the men answered.

"Wait until I get dressed."[1]

Pattie, fifty-six, had been the jailer for thirteen years. He went downstairs with a lantern and the keys to the cells. When he unlocked the front door,

Waterloo Turnpike, which the lynchers used to enter Warrenton. The undated postcard is probably from the early twentieth century. *Virginia Museum of History and Culture.*

the men pushed past him with the "prisoner," a man who appeared to Pattie to be Black.

As he moved to the courtyard between the two jail buildings, Pattie realized that it had filled with men, far too many to bring a prisoner to jail. Instead of unlocking the cell building, he turned and went back upstairs to his residence.

"I got to get my keys," he said.

Six men followed him.

"Are you going to take charge of this prisoner?"

"Let me see your papers."

"Take the prisoner, and we'll give you our papers."

In the darkness of his apartment, Pattie slipped the keys from his pocket and hid them on the mantel. He hoped the men had not seen him, but one did and plucked the keys from their hiding place.

"If you won't lock this man up, we will," he said.

Two men grabbed Pattie, one at each side, and the group marched back downstairs.

"Now that we have him in our power, tell him what we want," one said.

"We want Arthur Jordan," said another, drawing his pistol. "Do what we say, keep quiet, and you won't get hurt."

Above: The Fauquier History Museum at the Old Jail in Warrenton, a national and state historic landmark, where the Jordan lynching began. *Author's collection*.

Right: Cell at the Fauquier History Museum at the Old Jail. Jordan was abducted from the jail and lynched nearby in the town cemetery. *Author's collection*.

Jordan had been in the jail for about four days, charged with "taking a white woman from her home." Pattie said later that he did not recognize the men in the dim light; all but two of them were masked. He told the men he was afraid they would get the wrong prisoner or let the other inmates out.

"We know Jordan. There'll be no mistake," one said.

A tall man told his fellows, "Take charge of the old man while we go in and get Jordan." Four of them took hold of Pattie.

The others moved toward the cells, each about twelve feet by eighteen feet, with a small stove and wood-plank walls and ceilings. A cell could hold up to ten prisoners, but this night there were only three. Jordan lay on a blanket by the stove.

A man unlocked the cell.

"Arthur Jordan?"

"Here I am."

"Get up."

NOT A TRADITIONAL ROMANCE

J ordan faced the murderous mob in his jail cell because of what had happened months earlier at the farm where he worked in northern Fauquier County, Virginia.

Jordan had worked at Nathan Corder's farm for about two years when he began a romance with his employer's daughter, Elvira Corder. Their relationship was cursed, however, because he was Black and she was white.

Elvira was twenty-five, single and the oldest child and only daughter of Nathan and Bettie Corder. She was pretty and independent, with a competence born of dawn-to-dusk farmwork.

Arthur, also twenty-five, was said to be a good worker, but he too had a confidence about him that some white people described as arrogance.

Their relationship was complicated by the fact that Arthur was married and had an infant daughter. More importantly, this was rural Virginia, fifteen years removed from the Civil War, with a newly liberated Black population seeking opportunity and white residents determined to retain their standing. The romance was not to be.

We are unable to recover the details of their encounter. We have no letters, diaries or family accounts to tell of their dreams. But we can look to their actions and to the world in which they lived to fill in the gaps and to discover much of what must have happened.

Theirs could not have been a traditional romance. As a married Black man, he would not have enjoyed Sunday dinners with Elvira and her family or summer nights with her on the porch. This was a clandestine affair, illicit by law and custom and more likely to feature a secret embrace than an evening walk.

They must have been hesitant lovers at first, given the dangers, and then enthusiastic, given all that followed. It's not clear how long they were intimate, probably for several months.

If they were careful, the couple could conceal their romance. As historian Martha Hodes has noted, southern white women knew that if they had an affair with a Black man, he wouldn't say anything for fear of being killed. "The woman has only to avoid being impregnated and it is all safe," she wrote.[2]

But Elvira did become pregnant. One can imagine how she experienced symptoms, such as morning sickness or a missed period, surprising at first, but later recognized for what they were. She must have known that soon the dresses she wore would not hide her swelling shape, that her secret would not last. If she did not act, she would have to face her family, whose shame and rage were certain. "How could you be so foolish?" they might ask. "How could you do this to us?"

There must have been a private moment between the couple that began with Elvira saying in effect, "Arthur, I'm going to have a baby," followed by a desperate question: "What are we going to do?"

Marriage was one possibility if both were white, but it was inconceivable for a mixed-race couple. Besides, Arthur was already married.

Abortion was another possibility. The procedure had been illegal in Virginia for more than thirty years, though it was available in other states, such as North Carolina. If she could find someone to do it, Elvira would have to be away from the farm for a while, and she might need time to recover. How would she explain all this to her friends and family?[3]

The use of plants and medicines to induce an abortion also was a possibility. Yet there is nothing to indicate that Elvira was disposed toward abortion. At twenty-five, she was three years older than the average age for first-time brides in Fauquier.[4] Many women her age had already started their families. "In a few Eastern cities, the 'woman bachelor,' as she called herself, gained steadily in standing and public respect, [but] in most parts of the country, the 'elderly girl' was looked upon as a creature of frustrated purpose," said historian Arthur Meier Schlesinger.[5]

The South lost more than 100,000 men during the Civil War, reducing the pool of possible marriage partners. Said historian Peter Wallenstein, "Some white women were more likely than they would have otherwise been to look for marriage partners across the racial divide."[6]

We have no way of knowing for sure, but the warmth of Arthur's attentions may have been new to Elvira. It is possible that she was inexperienced at love, intoxicated by it and enjoying all aspects of it, including the arrival of a baby.

For Arthur, one wonders if Elvira's news inspired a moment of regret. Why had he pursued her? If she was the pursuer, why had he agreed to her advances? Was he at risk if he refused her? He was a husband and new father; she was a young white woman, the farmer's daughter. He must have known that if he touched her, disaster would follow.

Yet they continued. They had violated state laws against interracial intimacy; her pregnancy gave testimony to that. It is likely that they developed a deep love for one another. The attraction was apparently so strong that they were willing to give up their families and run a deadly risk to be together.

Faced with Elvira's news, Arthur chose not to flee without her, to abandon her and his family and start a new life elsewhere. Instead, he and Elvira decided to flee together, perhaps to give themselves time to resolve their dilemma.

The couple were young and unafraid, undaunted by the barriers erected by white men to constrain women and Black people. But they were also misguided and clung to the fanciful notion that in 1880 Virginia they could flee the Corder farm and live happily ever after. As English professor Suzanne W. Jones has noted, when novelists of the nineteenth and early twentieth centuries told stories of interracial romance, they often described them as "tragic impossibilities" with an "irresolvable conflict, often ending in death." It is an apt portrayal of Arthur and Elvira.[7]

But Elvira had a new life growing within her, driving her on, driving her away. Her pregnancy would soon expose the intolerance and cruelty within her family and her world. As with Arthur, flight was her only hope. She would try to reconstruct her life elsewhere.

Christmas was normally a time of celebration for both the Corder and Jordan families. Arthur had married the former Anna Roe one year earlier during the Christmas season. And two of Elvira's brothers and her stepmother had Christmastime birthdays. But that year, 1879, must have been without traditional cheer. Arthur and Elvira fled from Fauquier on a Saturday, just two days after the holiday.

The couple had planned their flight carefully. They went by train, first to Alexandria, Virginia, and then Washington, D.C. They left their homes at different times; took different routes; boarded the same eastbound train

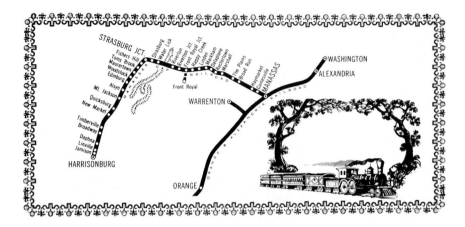

from different stations at Markham and Marshall; sat in separate cars, as the law required; and only when they reached their destination did they join together. She had secretly saved money for the trip, and like Shakespeare's Jessica, she stole money from her father. In all, she had nearly $1,000, or almost $28,000 today, when they left.

Back at Wheatfields, the family farm, chaos must have greeted the news of Elvira's absence. We can hear family members asking, "When did she leave?" "Does Father know?" and "What did he say?"

The family apparently knew nothing of the relationship but realized later that clues to the ripening romance were apparent all along. One of Elvira's jobs on the farm was to care for the cows. Each afternoon, she drove them into the barn and milked them. Only after she fled did the family realize that Elvira was later and later finishing the milking and returning to the house for supper. And Arthur had insisted on carrying the milk pails to the dairy, some distance from the house. The family thought little of these changes at first, but they made sense later when the storm broke.

Nathan must have been furious when he learned she was gone. The Corders were recognized by their neighbors as a respectable, hardworking and well-to-do family. But Elvira's disappearance meant dishonor and a failure for Nathan. He was unaware of what his daughter was planning and unable to prevent it.

We have no way of knowing what Elvira was thinking during this period. We don't know the options she considered or the time she spent in weighing those options. She was twenty-five and may not have seen clearly all the possible consequences. We do know, however, that her romance and flight were radical choices. She was expected to show restraint, abstinence and, most of all, submission. But she had rejected all that was expected of her.

Southern Railroad Depot, Marshall, Va.

Opposite: Arthur and Elvira boarded the same train, one from Markham and the other from Marshall, on their way to Washington. *Fauquier Heritage and Preservation Foundation.*

This page, top: What remains of the Markham train station. *Author's collection.*

This page, bottom: The Marshall train station. *Fauquier Heritage and Preservation Foundation.*

Above: The main house at Wheatfields. *Author's collection.*

Opposite: Wheatfields, in northern Fauquier County, was home to the Corder family for more than forty years. *Author's collection.*

"Southern white women were legally subordinated to and economically dependent on their fathers and husbands," said historian Crystal N. Feimster. "They had little choice but to accept paternalistic domination in exchange for male protection and a measure of discrete power within the household."[8]

Added Dr. James Norcom, a North Carolina physician, later exposed as a licentious slave master, "God in his inscrutable wisdom has appointed a place and a duty for the females, out of which they can neither accomplish their destiny nor secure their happiness."[9]

Elvira had rebelled against her expected place and duty. She had indulged her desires and now was tarnished. She was the unchaste daughter and exposed herself and her family to public censure.

As Atticus Finch said of Mayella Ewell, a white woman who made sexual advances toward Tom Robinson, a Black man, in *To Kill a Mockingbird*: "She has committed no crime, she has merely broken a rigid and time-honored code of our society, a code so severe that whoever breaks it is hounded from our midst as unfit to live with."[10]

One indication of this disgrace can be seen in a decision by the local weekly newspaper, the *True Index*. Its editor understood that readers would be interested in the story, so about two weeks after the couple's flight, the paper reported on their disappearance, how she had stolen money from her father, and how Arthur had abandoned his wife and child for "the erring girl." But the paper also decided that the details were just too sordid. It said that Elvira "brought the gray hairs of an old father in sorrow down to the grave," but added, "Out of sympathy for his distressed family, we suppress names."[11]

3

NOT ONE BUT TWO LETTERS

After reaching Washington, D.C., Arthur and Elvira headed west, probably by train, to western Maryland, near the Pennsylvania border. They stopped at the Shupp farm, just north of the town of Williamsport.

But why? Why did the couple choose Williamsport? Did Arthur know Abraham Shupp or Charles Shupp, his son, who farmed near his father? Did he know they would offer refuge? Perhaps, like many Black residents of Virginia before him, he believed he could find more opportunities north of the Potomac River.

The couple was comfortable in their new home, living and working on the farm and often traveling the short distance into town. They were either indifferent or unaware of the attention they attracted when they made these trips. This was January 1880, and Maryland's prohibitions against interracial romance and marriage were just as strict and just as old as Virginia's. For many of the white people in the small town, the sight of a Black man and pregnant white woman, arm-in-arm, must have been both surprising and offensive. Their excursions proved to be more dangerous than the couple suspected.

One such excursion came soon after the new year, on January 4, when the Black residents of the region dedicated a new church in downtown Williamsport. The local paper reported that the dedication included "all the appropriate ceremonies" and that an "immense crowd of colored persons" attended the ceremony.[12]

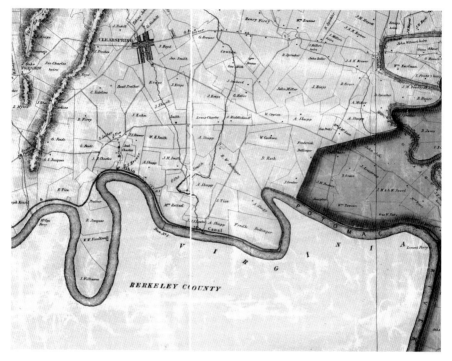

Arthur and Elvira lived at the Shupp farm. Abraham Shupp owned property near the Potomac River's Dam No. 5 and McCoy's Ferry. *Clear Spring Historical Association.*

Arthur and Elvira were among those in the crowd that Sunday morning. But they were noticed, either that day or later, by a man whose name was not recorded. We will call him the letter-writer. We know little about the letter-writer, except that he lived near Williamsport. We also know that he was upset to see Arthur and Elvira acting as if it was the most normal thing in the world for a mixed-race couple to enjoy an outing.

The more he learned about them, the more suspicious he became. He noticed that they appeared to have plenty of money. Soon he was convinced that they were running from something. As one newspaper reported, he decided that they were "acting in such a manner as to excite his suspicions that all was not right."[13]

The man either talked to the couple or asked about them and learned that they were from the village of Markham in northern Fauquier County, Virginia. He also learned that Arthur had once worked for a Mr. Triplett, a neighbor of Elvira's family. If Arthur and Elvira were hiding from her family, as he suspected, the family would want to know of his discovery.[14]

Dam No. 5 on the Potomac River between Maryland and West Virginia. *Author's collection.*

The man sent not one but two letters to Fauquier to report what he had seen. He sent one to Triplett, who lived in the village of Orlean, south of the Corder farm. He sent the second to the post office in Markham. The letter-writer didn't know Triplett or anyone in Fauquier. By sending two letters, he must have believed that he would improve the chances that his message of alarm would reach the right person.

His letters gave his name and location and added, "Arthur Jordan, a negro, accompanied by a white girl arrived here a few days ago and states that he has been living in Virginia and working for Mr. Triplett." The letters were spare of details, but they accomplished their purpose. Either Triplett, someone at the post office or both forwarded them to Nathan Corder, Elvira's father.[15]

There is no evidence that the family offered a reward for information about the couple or had suspected they were in Maryland. Their discovery by a stranger and his report to her family were much simpler than that. It was a matter of chance. The couple had been spotted by a man who was offended by the sight of them and moved to do something about it.

The man did not report Arthur and Elvira to the local police, or if he did, there's no evidence that they acted on his information. Instead, he took it upon himself to enforce the community's ban on interracial love, to meddle in a matter that did not directly involve him. He was, like the

Abraham Shupp, whose family housed and employed Arthur and Elvira, is buried near Clear Spring, Maryland. *Author's collection.*

mob that later confronted Jordan in the Warrenton jail, a self-appointed guardian of the status quo.

In December 1879, on the day the couple fled, Nathan tracked his daughter to the Markham rail station and, believing that he was close behind her, persuaded a conductor to delay a departing train so he could search the cars. He was too late; they were gone. On Monday a few days after Christmas, he tried again to find them, taking a train east to Alexandria, Virginia, and then Washington.

Nathan carried a pistol as he pursued the couple. At the Alexandria rail station, he learned that, yes, a young woman matching Elvira's description had been there and that she had gone on to Washington. Nathan followed but did not find them. He stopped again in Alexandria on the return trip and talked to a policeman.

"I promised my wife that I would bring her home dead or alive," he said, then softened his attitude a bit, at least toward his daughter. "I never wanted to murder anybody, but I will certainly kill the negro if I get the chance."[16]

The policeman would later describe Nathan as angry and "nearly heartbroken at the disgrace of his child." He suggested that Nathan end his search and return home, which he did.

It was apparent that Arthur's alliance with Elvira was consensual, that she had strong feelings for him. But Nathan refused to believe that. He believed that Arthur was the aggressor and blamed him for the Corders' shame. When Shakespeare wrote of an interracial romance, the angry father in his story said his daughter, Desdemona, had tied her "duty, beauty, wit and fortunes" to the "sooty bosom" of a Black man.[17]

Arthur and Elvira had tasted of new possibilities, a life together, yet their flight also revealed the true nature of their society, the violent intolerance. Their liaison was deemed subversive by the ruling caste, and it provoked what would become a murderous response. As one of Nathan's supporters said later, "Any attempt to contaminate the Anglo-Saxon shall be treated with severe remedies." Said another, Arthur's crime "is one that must call forth the unmeasured indignation of all right-thinking people."[18]

For the Corders, the letters appear to be the first word they had received about Elvira and Arthur since they departed. Nathan had several options when he finally learned where his daughter was hiding. He could have ignored the news about her, abandoning her to fend for herself. He also could have traveled to Maryland or sent one of his sons to check on her.

Perhaps, though, he had only one option. His neighbors might have understood if he turned his back on her. But would they have considered that sufficient? Would he? Something more ferocious was called for. As one news account said, "Upper Fauquier is very much stirred by an elopement of a negro man with a daughter of Mr. Nathan Corder, one of its most respectable citizens, for the purpose of marriage."[19]

Elvira was an adult, but Nathan did not consider what she wanted. It was as if he understood the tragedy that was unfolding—a classic tale of forbidden love—and the essential role that he played. He would go to Maryland to confront the couple. Now, with the letter-writer's information, he would have his revenge.

When Nathan first learned of Elvira's departure, his pursuit of her seemed impulsive and was ultimately unsuccessful. This time he would be more deliberate. Williamsport was two days' ride, and he had to assume Arthur and Elvira would not welcome his arrival. He needed a plan, and he needed help.

It would not be surprising if Nathan had to look on a map to find Williamsport, since the town had no obvious connection to Fauquier or to the Corder family. If he did, he would have seen that it was north of Fauquier, about eighty miles away, in western Maryland.

Williamsport was a busy river town on the east bank of the Potomac River. To the west were the mountains. To the east, one hundred miles away, was Baltimore. The town had about 1,500 residents and a prosperous commercial sector, with general stores, a clothing store, a drugstore, a jeweler, harness shops, livery stables, a weekly newspaper, physician offices and an undertaker. Residents worshipped at the Lutheran, Presbyterian and Catholic churches.

The town was founded in the eighteenth century near major travel routes, including two of the nation's earliest highways, the east–west National Pike and the north–south Great Wagon Road. It was also served by several rail lines and by the C&O Canal. The Shupp family had farmed the land north of town for many years.

The region was remarkably similar in appearance to northern Fauquier and must have reminded Arthur and Elvira of their home. Agriculture was the primary industry in both localities, as farmers raised grains, vegetables, fruit and livestock for markets to the east. And both were fertile valleys, standing in the shadow of the Appalachian foothills. The region had almost twice as many people as Fauquier and was 92 percent white.

By recruiting his neighbors to help him, Nathan added a political and cultural context to his dispute with his daughter. What started as a private family matter was now public. The community, or at least the white males of prominence, would help him enforce the ancient barriers.

He invited his neighbors to his home to tell them what he had learned. Several volunteered to ride north with him. News reports do not agree on exactly how many men joined him. Accounts varied from "a party of six of the best men in the neighborhood" to the "body of eight horsemen" who arrived in Williamsport.

The consensus seems to be that seven men set out from Markham in pursuit of the couple. They included Nathan, his older sons—John Corder, twenty-two, and Will Corder, twenty—and four neighbors.

The men who answered Nathan's call were men like him, independent and prosperous farmers. They were men of influence, members of long-standing Virginia families. They were men for whom personal honor and civic duty were important.

Unlike Nathan, several had fought for the Confederacy in the Civil War. It was as if they had been handpicked for this undertaking, men of action and command, accustomed to the hardships of a long ride. As one Fauquier veteran wrote after the war, the Confederate soldier had marched and fought "with nothing but a small ration of corn meal and coarse pork for his diet and with worthless money for his scant pay." Though now fifteen years older, these men must have seen this assignment as something they could and must accomplish. They were united in retribution and in defense of the community's honor, drawn by what sociologist Mattias Smångs has described as the "fellowship of the hunt."[20]

The men must have understood that they had volunteered for a task that would require them to cross a state line and kidnap two adults, to shackle one and force his return to Fauquier. And they feared no repercussions for what they were about to do. They would show that this was still a white man's country. They knew that their white neighbors would approve.

Two newspaper accounts at the time, including one in the *Alexandria Gazette*, mentioned the men by name. The *Gazette* was a regional daily with correspondents and readers in Fauquier. Its editors devoted unusual space to the Arthur and Elvira incident, publishing seven stories over a month, including stories on four consecutive days.

The *Gazette*'s story of January 21, 1880, named the men who rode with Nathan as Robert Stribling, Jaquilin Marshall Jr., Wallace J. Payne and his brother, John Rice Payne. One name in particular—that of Robert Stribling—must have stood out to Fauquier readers. Stribling, forty-six, was a Civil War hero, leader of the Fauquier Artillery and a former prisoner of war.[21]

In civilian life, he was a physician and the son of a physician, who lived just north of Nathan at "Mountain View" near Markham. He had been trained at the University of Virginia and the University of Pennsylvania and had just been elected to his first term in the Virginia House of Delegates. To have someone of Stribling's stature associated with the mission would have signaled the cooperation and permission of the highest local authority.

Unfortunately for the newspaper, its story on this point was wrong. The Virginia General Assembly was in session in January 1880, including the five days that the riders were either on the road or in Maryland. Stribling cast a dozen recorded votes during this period, including once when he rose to complain that he and others had departed the state capitol, thinking the day's business was done, only to learn later that the delegates had worked into the night. Stribling, who went on to serve multiple terms in the assembly, could not have been among those who abducted Jordan.

A second newspaper account may shed light on the *Gazette*'s error. The *Loudoun Mirror*, a weekly based in Leesburg, Virginia, near Fauquier, reported that one of the riders was J.B. Stribling, presumably Jacob Stribling, a twenty-nine-year-old neighbor of Nathan's. The *Gazette* identified the wrong Stribling.[22]

Another prominent name listed among the riders was Jaquilin Ambler Marshall. It's not clear if this referred to the fifty-year-old father or his twenty-one-year-old son with the same name. The Marshalls were neighbors of Nathan Corder and members of a large, illustrious Virginia family. "There had been Marshalls and Amblers present in the state since the earliest Colonial days; these were the first families," said historian Madeleine Forrest. The elder Marshall was the grandson of Chief Justice John Marshall and had been a justice of the peace in Fauquier.[23]

After the war, Jaquilin Marshall had to apply for a pardon from President Andrew Johnson under Johnson's "13th exception" to his general amnesty program. Most soldiers and citizens of the South were directly pardoned after the war, but Johnson made an exception for the wealthiest southerners. Those who were worth more than $20,000 in 1860, or about $700,000 today, had to apply for a pardon and swear allegiance to the Union. In insisting on this exception, Johnson singled out the South's landed gentry, the men, he reasoned, who had encouraged and financed the rebellion.

In his application, Marshall tried to counter this idea, saying that he had been opposed to secession but then joined the great majority of his neighbors in Fauquier and throughout Virginia in voting for it. "My occupation is and always has been that of a farmer," he wrote. "I have done nothing which would debar one from the benefits of the general amnesty."[24]

Wallace J. Payne, thirty-eight, and his younger brother, John Rice Payne, thirty-four, had ridden with the famed Company A, Seventh Regiment, Virginia Cavalry of the Army of Northern Virginia. Colonel Turner Ashby commanded the unit. Both men were wounded during the war. The Confederacy also reimbursed Wallace Payne for two of his horses killed in action, one at Brandy Station and the other at Upperville.[25]

The riders departed Fauquier on Monday, January 12, 1880, and rode north through today's Loudoun and Frederick Counties, into West Virginia. By early Tuesday, the horsemen had reached Charlestown, West Virginia, about forty miles from home.

Seven armed strangers, riding hard on what one observer said were "magnificent" horses, attracted considerable attention. In Charlestown, a news story described the men as "well-mounted, over-coated and supplied with revolvers." In Winchester, Virginia, they were described as "bold and daring fellows." In Williamsport, they reminded residents of "ye war times,"

The men who abducted Arthur and Elvira attracted press attention wherever they went, as this front-page story from Hagerstown, Maryland, shows. *Author's collection.*

fifteen years earlier, when Union and Confederate soldiers marched through town. "They were neither foraging or scouting," the local paper said. "They were in search of a runaway couple—a negro man and a white girl."[26]

In Charlestown, they arrived at 3:00 a.m. and rousted the proprietor of the City Hotel, who took them in. They stayed but a few hours, and before leaving, they went to a local store to buy pistol cartridges. When one of the men carelessly handled his weapon, the pistol discharged, sending a ball through his hand. One can imagine the loud crash of the pistol, the screams of the injured man and the chaos that followed. "Dr. J.D. Starry rendered the necessary surgical attention," the local paper reported.[27]

The calamity punctured the air of mystery and menace that surrounded the mounted men and replaced it with comic ineptitude. Even so, there was a lethal momentum about them as they continued their ride.

The riders crossed the Potomac River, as did many north–south travelers, on Lemen's Ferry. The ferry ran from the West Virginia shore to the town of Williamsport. During the Civil War, a Union engineer reported that the ferry was capable of carrying dozens of soldiers at a

Lemen's Ferry connected West Virginia with Williamsport. The men who kidnapped Arthur and Elvira used it to reach them. *Williamsport Area Historical Association.*

An artist's rendering of Lemen's Ferry and its connection to the town of Williamsport. *Williamsport Area Historical Association.*

time, so these seven horsemen posed no problem. The ferry was held in place by a shore-to-shore overhead cable, running on wheels. The trip across took about three minutes.

In Williamsport, the men stayed the night with the letter-writer. He had been the impetus for their journey, and he helped them again the next morning by showing the way to the Shupp farm.

When the riders arrived at the farm, they surprised Jordan in the barn, where he was cleaning the stables. He was surrounded, "strongly bound," shoved toward the horses and forced to mount. Newspapers reported that he did not resist. Yet that seems unlikely, given his cries for help later in Winchester and Warrenton. He said later that he initially thought the riders were a legitimate posse, arrived from his home with a warrant for his arrest.

When Elvira saw the men, she understood instantly the implications. Her lover and the father of her unborn child was being forced to return to Fauquier. She must have understood that he would probably be killed. One account said she was "very indignant at such proceedings and refused to be comforted although one of the young gentlemen did all in his power to console her."[28]

Elvira's resistance may have forced the riders to change their plans. They may have intended to return to Fauquier with both Arthur and Elvira. But her anger appears to have been spontaneous and unexpected. They could not risk the long ride home with both of them.

Instead, one of them took her back to Williamsport and placed her in the Taylor Hotel. Newspapers reported that the family intended to return to the hotel for Elvira and travel home by train because of her "delicate" condition.

William Taylor, the hotel proprietor, was fifty-two, and a native of Fairfax, Virginia. He was a former boatman on the canal, a widower and the father of eight children. He was also a southern sympathizer, and according to present-day relatives, he would not have approved of what Elvira had done or allowed her to stay long in his hotel.[29]

Taylor was said to have won the hotel in a poker game during the Civil War. The owner was afraid that the Union army would burn the town, so he offered the hotel as ante in the card game. Taylor won the hand, the town was spared and Taylor refused to sell back the hotel to the owner.

The hotel had at least one famous visitor. General Robert E. Lee, retreating with his troops from the Battle of Gettysburg in 1863, was said to have sat on a sandstone block in front of the hotel and talked to local residents before heading south across the river.

The Taylor Hotel is gone now but was located in downtown Williamsport. *Williamsport Area Historical Association.*

Elvira's resistance at the Shupp farm gave lie to two claims made about her when she and Arthur fled, that she was dim-witted and that she was a victim. She had spent a lifetime watching and listening to her father. Nathan had followed the couple all the way from Fauquier to correct what he saw as a grievous wrong. That morning at the barn, she understood instantly what was happening and the risks to Arthur and herself, and she tried to prevent them.

Her actions, including her visits to Williamsport, also refuted the notion that Arthur had forced himself on her and had insisted that she run away with him. That morning she did not act like a prisoner being freed from captivity. She was not grateful or relieved to see her family. She was angry.

Arthur's abduction in Maryland brought to mind the infamous international slave trade. Like a captured African from decades earlier, he was suddenly bound, dragged from his home and carried against his will to a distant place of imprisonment. His kidnapping was also reminiscent of what happened to runaway slaves under the Fugitive Slave Act, when owners or slavecatchers ran down their human quarry and returned them to captivity.

With Arthur as their prisoner, the men rode south from the Shupp farm, crossed the Potomac River to West Virginia and headed for home. They had ridden about thirty-five miles when they arrived in Winchester, Virginia, a

The Potomac River site where McCoy's Ferry used to be. Arthur's abductors probably used this ferry to return home with their captive. *Author's collection.*

county seat and regional market in the Shenandoah Valley, with three times as many people as Warrenton.

Even so, a party of six white men leading a shackled Black man attracted attention. One account said the men "pranced" down Loudoun Street, confident and apparently unaware that Jordan would soon make his abduction more difficult.[30]

When the captors stopped at Robinson Hardware, Jordan started screaming.

"Help!" he cried. "Police."

The screams drew a crowd, including Town Constable Smith and Policeman Brown. Two of the riders, sensing trouble, whipped Jordan's horse and tried to leave town, but Smith stopped them. Jordan cried out that he was being kidnapped and asked for a lawyer.

"Help me," he said again.

When the riders could not produce a warrant, Smith took everyone to see Justice Crebs. Meanwhile, several Black people who had heard Jordan's pleas raced for a lawyer.

Crebs heard their stories and sided with the white men. He blamed Jordan for what had happened and excused Corder for doing what any father would do. The mixing of the races was illegal in Virginia, he reasoned, and had to be punished.

The fact that the men had violated the law themselves by kidnapping Jordan was a technicality Crebs easily solved by deputizing one of the riders and issuing a warrant for Jordan. Crebs instructed the men to deliver Jordan to the Warrenton jail, and the men promised they would.

Meanwhile, Black residents found an attorney, but when they reached Crebs's office, the riders, with Arthur in tow, were gone. The Black residents of town were said to be "greatly excited" and predicted that Jordan would be lynched.[31]

The incident in Winchester, though it probably took less than an hour, illustrated what would become a decades-long reality for Black residents of Virginia. With emancipation, the end of the Civil War and the passage of the Thirteenth, Fourteenth and Fifteenth Amendments, Black males, at least, could hope to become full citizens in a democratic system. In this case, as they raced to find an attorney, the Black residents of Winchester must have hoped that their efforts would be worthwhile. But little had changed. If these white men wanted to kidnap a Black man, cross a state line and later hang him, nobody was going to stop them.

VOLUNTARY AND CLANDESTINE

T here are no photos of Elvira, no letters or diaries, no clue as to what she was like. What we know of her appearance and character comes from news accounts published after she became pregnant and ran away with Arthur. Those accounts agree that she was an attractive young woman, small and buxom. We can picture her in a full-length cotton work dress, with long sleeves and high neck, seated on a wooden stool in the barn, milking the cows. She was "fine-looking," said one account. "Exceedingly pretty," said another.[32]

But each compliment was paired with a condescending assessment of her abilities. She was "half-witted," "simple in her intellect" and "laboring for some time under great mental depression." It was as if the reporters, in reflecting the feelings of the community, had to believe she was "easily misled and overcome." Only then could they begin to understand why a young white woman would leave her family and home to run away with a married Black man.[33]

Elvira was born in 1855 in Fauquier, the oldest child and only daughter of Nathan and Bettie Corder. She was big sister to brothers John and Will. Elvira's parents lost a baby daughter when Elvira was two, and Bettie died when Elvira was about nine.

Nathan remarried soon after, this time to a wealthy widow and distant relative, Elizabeth Corley. When Elizabeth joined the household, she brought with her Ann, fifteen, and William, thirteen, the two children she had with her first husband. She and Nathan had two more children: Ada, who died as an infant, and Charles.

Elvira's duties in the home, on the farm and in the care of her younger brothers probably increased after her mother's death and may have become more difficult with the arrival of Elizabeth and her children. Was Elizabeth the evil stepmother and Ann the demanding stepsister?

We know little of Elvira's relationship with Elizabeth, though the two must not have been close. Years later, with Ann married and moved away, Elvira began her ill-fated relationship with Arthur. Elizabeth was just as surprised and embarrassed as everyone else when that romance exploded into view and, given Nathan's statements later, just as angry. It would be interesting to know if Elvira had a close female friend, an intimate to confide in, someone who could have warned her. The Corders often had others living with them on their farm, but by 1880, the only boarders were two farmhands, Inman Payne and Ed Utterback.

Elvira attended school at least until age fourteen and could read and write. But her world appears to have been limited and isolated, typical of life in the small farms and villages of rural Virginia. There is no evidence that she ever married, held a job, lived anywhere but on the farm or did anything but farmwork.

Given this life, it is fair to ask if Elvira was happy. Did her romance, pregnancy and flight suggest a cruelty in the household? How did she feel about her father, her brothers and her stepmother? Was she lonely? Did young men from the neighborhood seek her attentions? Her stepsister, Ann, was married at age twenty-one to Elisha Booten Corder, Nathan's nephew. One wonders if there were any "country cousins" for Elvira to marry.

Elvira grew up at a time when Fauquier was a majority-Black county, due in part to what was one of Virginia's largest slave populations. The county had 10,455 enslaved people in 1860, plus 821 free Black people, outnumbering the 10,430 white residents.[34]

Elvira's father and two uncles farmed together with the work of enslaved people. John Corder, their grandfather, owned slaves, bequeathing them to his family as callously as he did his feather bed. He specified in his will that his wife was to receive one cow, one bed, their furniture and "one black man Frank and one black woman named Beck." The remaining ten slaves that he owned were to be equally divided among his children "according to lot and valuation."[35]

Nathan's mother owned a slave, and the Corder brothers owned and rented enslaved people, including children under age fourteen. That meant that the Corder farm was awash with children, including Elvira's cousins, but also the children of the enslaved people.

Elvira's upbringing may have contributed to the dramatic events of her later life. As the daughter of a yeoman farmer, she would have experienced long hours of toil and responsibility. She probably knew how to hitch a plow and where to find the best pond ice. And she would have done this work and gained this knowledge in the company of Black people, both enslaved and free. Her relationships with the resident Black workers would have been a complicated one, but she probably enjoyed a comfort or ease around them.

In running away with Arthur, she displayed some of the same qualities needed on the farm, like initiative and independence. She also chose the forbidden with its intoxicating mix of joy and rebellion. But these feelings hid a fearful future, for theirs was a condemned love.

A decade later, Black journalist and civil rights advocate Ida Wells-Barnett wrote that southern white men refused to recognize a voluntary association between a white woman and a Black man, insisting instead that the fact of an encounter was proof of force. Said historian Crystal N. Feimster, "The mere suggestion that a white woman would willingly consent to sex with a black man was enough to send white men into violent hysterics."[36]

In Elvira's case, this can be seen in news accounts of her romance. Readers were told that she was Jordan's "inamorata," or lover, and that he forced himself on her and threatened to kill her if she told her family. He violated her night after night throughout the summer and fall, news accounts said, until she became pregnant. Finally, he insisted that she run away with him to Maryland. "Made wild with grief and shame," she consented, one story said.[37]

Missing from these narratives is any possibility that their association was what Wells-Barnett would characterize as voluntary, clandestine and illicit. "There are white women in the South who love the Afro-American's company, even as there are white men notorious for their preference for Afro-American women," she wrote.[38]

Elvira's actions, especially her unmarried pregnancy, hint at some sort of dysfunction within her family. It's possible her relationship with Arthur was in some way a rebellion against her father. Or she may have simply enjoyed Arthur's affections.

We have no direct accounts to give insight into Elvira's thinking about Arthur. But we can gain insight from the experience of Ruth McBride, a young white woman, and her romance with a young Black man named Peter. More than fifty years separate the two love stories, yet they are surprisingly similar and follow the pattern described by law professor Sheryll Cashin. "To love beyond boundaries is the most radical of acts. It also requires optimism," she wrote.[39]

Ruth and Peter lived at a time and place—Suffolk, Virginia, in 1936—when a Black-white relationship was discouraged if not forbidden by law. Ruth and her family operated a grocery store adjacent to one of the city's Black neighborhoods.[40]

One day, Peter invited Ruth to go for a walk, and Ruth accepted. "He was a bold guy because from that moment he was risking his life," she told her son in an interview. "God knows what I was thinking about. The only thing I told him was, 'If my father sees us, we're in trouble.'"

Ruth fell in love with Peter, and the couple had sex. "He was the first man other than my grandfather who ever showed me any kindness in my life, and he did it at the risk of his own, because they would have strung him up faster than you can blink if they'd have found out," she recalled. "Not just the Ku Klux Klan but the regular white folks in town would've killed him."

The couple exchanged notes and had regular, secret rendezvous behind the store. "My whole life changed after I fell in love," she said. "It was like the sun started shining on me for the first time, and for the first time in my life I began to smile. I was loved, and I didn't care what anyone thought."

Soon Ruth was pregnant. She suggested that they run away together, but she could see that Peter was frightened. "If white folks find out you're pregnant by me, I will surely hang," he said.

Ruth thought no one knew about her romance and pregnancy, but she was wrong. Her mother had noticed and, one day, pulled Ruth aside to say, "Why don't you go to New York this summer to see your grandmother?"

Events in Elvira's life in 1879 followed a similar path. We can imagine the secret meetings and forbidden sex. We can appreciate Elvira's terror at discovering that she was pregnant, her loneliness in not being able to confide in anyone and her fear for Arthur and herself.

The differences between the two stories are profound, however. Elvira had no mother with whom to share her burden and no grandmother in New York to help her get an abortion. Elvira and Arthur were older and perhaps more confident than Ruth and Peter. They wanted to stay together but realized that they could not remain in Fauquier. In their case, however, flight didn't make right.

Ruth said she could not understand why white people were so opposed to a mixed-race romance. "I didn't give a hoot that he was black," she said. "He was kind. And good. I wanted to tell folks that. I actually believed folks would accept that, that they'd see what a good person he was and maybe accept us."

One can imagine Elvira thinking the same thing about Arthur, that he was a good man, that his race didn't matter, that people would like him once they got to know him.

But Ruth and Elvira were wrong. The differences did matter.

5

QUIET CONFIDENCE

As with Elvira, all we know of Arthur's appearance and character come from news accounts published after he and Elvira ran away. For that reason, some of them are suspect. For example, one account included several racist stereotypes in a single sentence when it described Jordan as a "large, bull-necked, thick-lipped negro, very black and forbidding-looking."[41]

However, stories in the *Alexandria Gazette*, the regional daily, written by their Fauquier correspondents, and one in the *Warrenton Solid South*, the local weekly, were more carefully drawn. One said Jordan was five ten, 160 pounds and "remarkably well-built." Another said, he was copper colored, "his hair was always well combed, and he generally presented a neat appearance."[42]

Arthur was the second child and oldest son born about 1855 to Henry and Lizzie Jordan. Like his father, he worked for local farmers as a laborer. He could not read or write and apparently had little schooling.

In Arthur, Elvira was attracted to a man who was the same age and, like her, a native of Fauquier. Yet their backgrounds were very different. Elvira grew up in the security of a large, extended family. Her experiences were limited but her life was stable, as she lived most of her life in one house. The Corders were not wealthy, but their farm was successful, and they grew, purchased or traded for whatever they needed.

Arthur, on the other hand, had lived a life of hardship and uncertainty. Even so, he seems to have endured and developed a maturity and sense of self that Elvira may have found attractive. Was she Desdemona, drawn to her Othello by the "dangers he had passed"?[43]

The Jordans were probably once enslaved people since there is no mention of them in early census records or in any listing of free Black people in Fauquier. When they do appear in the 1870 federal census, however, the family had scattered, apparently because of Henry's death. Arthur, sixteen, was on his own, living with seventeen other people, including the extended Peter King family and other unrelated adults. His mother, Lizzie, about forty, with her two youngest sons, James and Thomas, was living in the household of Thomas Diggs, working as the white family's domestic.

By 1880, Polly and Elizabeth, Arthur's sisters, were married and on their own. Arthur had been murdered early that year, and Polly, the oldest, named her first child Arthur, presumably in memory of her brother.

On the day after Christmas in 1878, the twenty-three-year-old Arthur married the former Anna Roe, twenty-one, also of Fauquier. The following year Anna gave birth to an infant daughter, Annie. The family lived in the Carter's Run Church section of the county, south of the Corder farm. Arthur had been working for the Corders for about two years when he and Elvira began their romance.[44]

Arthur was said to be reliable and hardworking and carried himself with a confidence that some white observers described as impudent. He was born during slavery's final chapter and would have been about ten years old when the Civil War ended, ushering in a new world of freedom for Black people. He would

A Negro Lynched and Hung.

A few weeks ago, a negro man, Arthur Jordan, who is married and has two children, and who had been in the employ of Mr. Nathan Corder, of Upper Fauquier, near Markham Station, ran off with a good-looking, half-witted daughter of Mr. Corder, aged about 17 years, whom he had before ruined, and went with her to Maryland.

On Wednesday week, a party of half a dozen men from the neighborhood where the parents lived went in search of the parties, and found them near Williamsport in Maryland. The girl was taken to Taylor's Hotel in that place, and placed under the care of the proprietor until her family could be notified, and the negro man was brought back to be confined in the Fauquier jail.

The party with the negro in charge passed through Winchester on Thursday week. The Winchester *News* says:

"The party of five persons and the negro, all on horseback, were proceeding through Loudoun street, when in front of Robinson's hardware store the negro refused to go any farther, and stated that he desired to see a lawyer. His captors tried to urge him in vain, when Constable Smith and Policeman Brown, attracted by the affair, arrested the whole party, negro and all, and carried them before Justice Crebs. Here a warrant was sworn out in form, and one of the party being a constable, the negro was delivered into his custody to be returned to Fauquier."

He was taken to Warrenton and confined in the jail of Fauquier county, on Friday night a week, but a large body of disguised men forced their way into the jail about 2 o'clock on the morning of Monday of last week, and took the prisoner, Arthur Jordan, and hung him on a tree near the cemetery about half a mile from Warrenton. The verdict of the jury of inquest was, in effect, that the victim came to his death by strangulation at the hands of from 40 to 60 men unknown to the jury,

In Staunton, Virginia, the *Spectator* devoted considerable space and prominence to coverage of Jordan's lynching. Many other papers did the same. *Author's collection.*

have grown up in this new climate, one in which young Black men rejected the rituals of submission and may have allowed themselves to dream of a better future. They were "undisciplined by slavery and unschooled in proper racial etiquette," wrote historian Leon F. Litwack. The white South had growing doubts that "this new generation could be trusted to stay in its place without legal and extra-legal force," he said.[45]

His defiance can be seen after his kidnapping in Maryland, when his captors returned with him to Fauquier, stopping in Orlean, a village just south of Markham and the Corder home. The *Gazette* correspondent was there to interview the prisoner, still bound hand and foot on horseback.

Jordan defended himself, saying he was not sorry for anything he had done. He said he had not staged a mock marriage ceremony with Elvira in Washington, as some had suspected. And he said that he had not violated any law, though her pregnancy cast doubt on that claim. The couple had run away on the one-year anniversary of his marriage to Anna. When told that Anna had been "thrown into spasms" when she learned that he had left her and their infant daughter, he is reported to have replied, "I don't care."

"He was very independent and indifferent to his fate, indignant," the story concluded.[46]

In fact, Jordan was defiant throughout his ordeal, from the time when he and his abductors were riding through Winchester, Virginia, to the moment in the Warrenton jail when mob members entered his darkened cell and asked for him. "Here I am," he replied. Later, as the mob dragged him toward the cemetery and his death, he continued to protest. Finally, one of the men silenced him.

This assurance, his unwillingness to be subservient, was noted in several accounts of Jordan's death and seems to have been just as galling to his white captors as his alliance with Elvira. He had loved a white woman, but he also had violated that absolute rule of white superiority.

FAMILY OF SLAVE OWNERS

N athan Corder, Elvira's father, hailed from one of the First Families of Virginia, though not as the title is usually used. The Corders did not acquire wealth or social status in the new colony, but they arrived from England in the 1600s and were among Virginia's earliest settlers.

John Corder, Nathan's grandfather, volunteered at age seventeen and served for more than two years with Virginia troops in the fight against the British during the Revolutionary War.

Nathan was the fifth of eleven children, born about 1818 to Elisha and Tacey Corder. The Corders were farmers and worked the land on both sides of the Rappahannock River in Fauquier and Rappahannock Counties. When Nathan was sixteen, several of his uncles decided that opportunities were greater to the west and joined a covered wagon train headed for Missouri. The caravan was three miles long when it left Flint Hill, Virginia. According to family lore, John Corder gave each of his sons $5,000 in cash, equipped their wagons with everything necessary and gave each of them four slaves.[47]

Nathan lived and farmed in Rappahannock County with his widowed mother and three of his siblings until Tacey's death from bronchitis after 1850. His father had died two decades earlier when Nathan was about ten, when the elder Corder fell from a horse and broke his neck. When his mother died, he moved to Fauquier to join his younger brother, Butler Corder, who had been renting farmland there. By then, Nathan was married to his cousin, the former Bettie Cowgill. They had one child, two-year-old Elvira, and Bettie was pregnant with their second child, John. A third, Will, would soon follow. The family lived on the Fauquier property for more than forty years in an eight-room, two-story farmhouse built about 1867.

Two years after Nathan started farming with Butler, a third brother, A.B. Corder, joined them. The three families lived next door to one another and numbered eighteen people, counting all the children and relatives.

Nathan was a former slave master, from a line of slave owners who reached back at least forty years. He lived in a state with more enslaved people than any other and in a county with an enslaved population of one enslaved person for every white person. In all, the Corder brothers had seventeen slaves, including nine children, on their farm.[48]

The brothers also did what many Fauquier farmers did: they rented enslaved people from their neighbors. For some slave masters, the hiring out of slaves was a lucrative business. The owner received a fee for the slave's labor, which the owner sometimes shared with the enslaved person. The person renting the slave would be responsible for the slave's keep. The hired slave would do the same labor as a nonhired slave. In all, the Corders rented five adults.

For example, Nathan paid Robert Corn, the administrator for the estate of Charles Jett of nearby Culpeper County, for the labor of a twenty-two-year-old female slave, who appears to have brought her children, ages three and one, with her.

Virginia slave owners routinely hired out slave women and children, and the practice was pervasive in rural areas, according to historian John J. Zaborney.

"Hired slave women with young children in Virginia everywhere faced arduous days, and they were forced to divide their time between care of their own children and labor for the white family that had hired them," Zaborney said.[49]

Each year, Fauquier County collected personal property tax from the brothers and all other local residents. Farmers, for example, paid taxes on their livestock, farm equipment, household possessions and the people they owned. In 1861, the brothers claimed five slaves, eight horses, thirty-five head of cattle, thirty sheep and thirty-two hogs.[50]

The brothers farmed together for about ten years but ended their joint venture soon after the Civil War when Butler and A.B. and their families moved away. Nathan reduced the amount of land he had under cultivation and continued to farm in the same location, near present-day Hume.

Nathan and Bettie were married for about nine years, until her death in 1864, when Nathan was forty-six and Bettie was thirty-nine. Nathan remarried soon after Bettie's death to Elizabeth Ball Corley, a thirty-four-year-old widow. They would remain married until his death almost thirty years later.

We have no photos of Nathan, no letters or diaries and few other sources to give hint as to his appearance or character. What we do know is that his upbringing and his actions tell of a man striving for self-sufficiency for himself and his family. Above him on the social/economic ladder were the wealthy planters who commanded large labor forces and substantial acreage. Below him were the poor white farmers who owned neither slaves nor land. Nathan was in the middle, with land he rented and then purchased; slaves, both rented and owned; hired hands; and family.

One newspaper account described the Corders as "plain, hard-working, honest people, who asked no favors, tilled the ground and paid their debts." It is telling that when Nathan experienced what he believed to be a family crisis, his friends and neighbors answered his call and followed him twice on missions of vengeance, first when they abducted Arthur and Elvira in Maryland and second when they killed Jordan in Warrenton.[51]

When Nathan died in 1892, his family listed his age on his tombstone as seventy-three years, ten months and nine days, as if each of those days was memorable. "A precious one from us has gone," the tombstone says. "A voice we love is stilled. A chair is vacant in our house."

But Nathan was also cruel, iron willed and unforgiving. His actions demonstrate support for Virginia's long history of discrimination and violence against Black people. To him, the color line between Black and white was not to be breached. When his oldest child and only daughter did so, he sacrificed her and his first grandchild to hateful notions of white superiority.

ROYAL HERITAGE

The land that drew the Corders to Fauquier County bore a royal heritage, part of a vast grant from King James II of England. The tract consisted of nearly 5.3 million acres that today encompasses twenty-three counties in Virginia and West Virginia. Thomas, the sixth Lord Fairfax, inherited much of the land before it eventually passed to a syndicate headed by John Marshall, later the nation's chief justice. James Marshall, John's brother, was part of the syndicate and on his death bequeathed his share to his children.

His son, also named James Marshall, inherited almost five thousand acres in Fauquier and Rappahannock Counties. Marshall leased five hundred acres to the Corders near present-day Hume, in Fauquier, sixty miles south and west of the nation's capital.

The region was a mix of forest and field, foothills and valley. To the west was the rugged terrain of the Blue Ridge Mountains; to the east, the fertile coastal plain. In that sense, it was a transition land, a land unto itself. The mountain gaps on the western edge of the county led to the development of paths and roads where residents could move west, and then to the establishment of a thriving agricultural economy since the roads offered a way to get the crops to market. The county was one of Virginia's smallest in population but one of the largest in acreage.

The county was then, and still is, an agricultural region, 651 square miles, and shaped like the cartoon silhouette of a French general with a flat hat and big nose. In Nathan's day, sheep and cattle outnumbered people, in part because the population had been declining for more than fifty years.

Left: John Marshall, former chief justice, was an early owner of what later became the Corder farm. His statue is at the courthouse in Warrenton. *Author's collection.*

Right: Thomas, the sixth Lord Fairfax, inherited thousands of acres in Virginia, including what later became the Corder farm. *Fauquier Heritage and Preservation Foundation.*

More than half of the residents worked the land or were connected to it, such as the plow maker who was one of Nathan's neighbors. Because of that, they worried about the same things, like the price of cattle in Baltimore and whether the fields were too wet to work.

These were the descendants of the earliest colonial families who had moved north and west from the Tidewater sections of the state. Because of their labor, the county was one of the state's breadbaskets. Whether the measure was bushels of wheat or pounds of wool, Fauquier was consistently among the state's top producers.

Most of the residents were natives of the county and Protestant by faith, primarily Baptist. Like the majority of voters throughout Virginia, they voted Democratic in the 1880 presidential election, supporting Winfield S. Hancock in his losing race against James A. Garfield. At life's end, Fauquier residents died primarily of consumption, a bacterial infection of the lungs now known as tuberculosis.

The ads in the *True Index*, the local weekly newspaper, tell of their isolation and aspirations. For example, J. Uhlfelder told readers that he had just returned from a buying trip to Baltimore, where he had obtained a "well selected stock of spring and summer" clothing, including fancy prints, exquisite notions and bleached muslin. He and R. Colinsky, the owner of

The rural landscape near Wheatfields, where the Nathan Corder family lived. *Author's collection.*

a competing dry goods store, said they accepted country produce, such as butter, eggs and chickens, "the chief currency of many of our people," in exchange for their merchandise.[52]

News stories at the time reported on the great technological and creative changes that were occurring elsewhere. Edison had just invented the first practical electrical light and Carnegie the first steel furnace. The typewriter and seismograph were new, and Pasteur had shown how to prevent the growth of the strep bacteria. Victoria was more than forty years into her reign as queen of England. Tchaikovsky was composing and Dostoevsky was writing. Stalin and Einstein had just been born. The United States included Virginia and thirty-seven other states.

In 1880, the county had about twenty-three thousand residents. Today, it is increasingly a bedroom community with seventy-three thousand people, many of whom are federal workers who commute to northern Virginia and Washington.

The landscape is remarkably similar to how it looked in Nathan's day. The Corders would recognize the historic road network; the settlements like Barbee's Crossroads, now Hume; and the patchwork of farms, orchards, pastures and hardwood forests.

To the north and west of their farm were mountains with colorful names like Hardscrabble, Rattlesnake and Little Cobbler. Streams like Fiery Run and Kettle Run provided fresh water and power for the gristmills and sawmills.

By the time the Corders arrived in Fauquier, a new railroad line had been built just north of their farm. Before then, farm products had to be hauled in wagons over muddy roads or by river to markets in Alexandria, Georgetown or Baltimore. Daily passenger service also was available, which would be how Arthur and Elvira fled the area.

The brothers were tenants on this land rather than owners. Typically, that meant that they paid a per-acre rent, as well as a share of what they produced. That arrangement lasted for more than a decade, until 1881, when Nathan paid $25 per acre to James Marshall's estate for 296 acres, the land he was already farming. He called his home Wheatfields.

The Corder farm was diversified, with revenues flowing from crops and livestock. On their best land, the family grew wheat, corn, rye and oats, which they sold for cash or fed to the animals. On the rolling, rocky sections, they grazed cattle, sheep and horses. Their herd of fifteen horses did the heavy work of the farm, such as the dragging of logs from the wood lot. One could also find hogs and chickens in the barnyard. Eggs, milk, butter, potatoes, honey and timber were important cash crops.

The cattle, sheep and hogs were short-term residents of Wheatfields. They arrived in late fall or early winter, through trade or purchase. Many were gone the following year. If the Corders had done their jobs well and enjoyed a bit of luck, the animals were bigger when they left Wheatfields, fattened by the corn and grasses.

A cow that weighed 700 pounds and cost $30 on arrival might weigh 1,100 pounds and be worth $45 when shipped for sale to nearby Marshall or distant markets in Baltimore. The cash difference helped finance all other aspects of the Corder farm, from a new saw to the sugar used at the breakfast table.

Like their neighbors, the Corders lived by the seasons: planting crops in April and May, tending them during the hot summer days and gathering their yield in fall. Yet each day, seven days a week, no matter the season or weather, they had to care for their animals. They were rulers of their rocky empire, but also prisoners of it, for it allowed little exposure to the world past their fields.

"Farmers had to raise most of what they as well as the animals ate," said Robert Beverly Herbert in his book about growing up on a Fauquier farm at the time. "This meant gardens had to be worked, cows had to be milked, wood had to be chopped, horses had to be provided and in fact most of what we lived on was home-raised."[53]

Nathan shared this work with his brothers, enslaved people and later with his children. His two older boys, John and Will, assumed major roles as they grew older. Elvira, too, helped inside the house and in the barns and gardens.

Lawrence Washington, a neighbor of Nathan's and a distant relative of the nation's first president, recorded in his farm diary at the time the almost infinite list of chores that farm families faced, from slaughtering hogs to clearing the fields of stones, thistle and oxeye. In October 1885, Washington carefully recorded that he sold J.W. Shackleford the apples from twenty-two trees for seventy-five cents per barrel, "he to pick them."[54]

Nathan also employed hired hands. A "year-hand" like Arthur typically earned about ten to twelve dollars per month. Many employers also set aside one cow and one hog for each employee, in addition to regular provisions known as "findings," such as meal, flour and pork.

Nathan and his brothers had been farming together about four years when the Civil War disrupted their lives. At first, many county residents feared secession and the start of a conflict, believing correctly that because of its location, Fauquier would be trampled beneath the engines of war. But when the idea of secession was finally put to a vote of the eligible white males in 1861, the vote was 1,809 in favor, 4 against.

Nathan was forty-four when the Confederacy began a draft to fill out its army. The first conscription included white males eighteen to thirty-five, to serve for three years. Within months, the new government expanded the draft pool to age forty-five. Butler Corder, Nathan's younger brother, served with the Forty-Third Battalion of the Virginia Cavalry, the famed Mosby's Rangers.[55] But Nathan avoided service, perhaps because of his age. Still, the war found him.

No major battles took place in Fauquier, though neighboring counties did host significant engagements, and forces from both sides crossed Fauquier many times. In addition, the county became what historian Madeleine Forrest calls "perhaps the most famous postage-stamp-sized piece of soil in the South," the Mosby Confederacy.[56]

Colonel John S. Mosby and his Rangers roamed northern Fauquier, Loudoun and other areas nearby, destroying, capturing or otherwise disrupting Union supplies and lines of communication. Fauquier residents supplied and sheltered the guerrilla unit. Mosby convalesced there after being shot by Union soldiers in 1864. Residents "saw Union soldiers killed and a general captured, railroads and supply trains interrupted and the enemy terrified," Forrest said.[57]

In addition, wounded from the battles of Manassas, Ball's Bluff, Fredericksburg and Chancellorsville arrived in Fauquier to be treated in makeshift hospitals. One of the county's most prominent landmarks, an obelisk erected in 1877 in the Warrenton Cemetery, marks a mass grave for six hundred Confederate soldiers killed at the Battles of First and Second Manassas. Three years after the memorial was placed, residents would drag Jordan past it to a nearby tree and hang him.

"Marching Confederate armies had to be fed with local farm produce, while the invaders merely took what they wanted," wrote John Keith, describing the Fauquier homefront. As a result, Fauquier was plundered. "To the armies, Fauquier was the land of milk and honey," added Forrest. "There was much to be taken from the rich fields filled with both crops and healthy livestock, from the well-stocked stores and from the stables which held well-bred horses. As a result, both armies plundered Fauquier many times."[58]

As in other wars, civilians had to endure a lack of food and clothing and a shortage of medicines and medical care. "They destroyed all our fence, all our orchard and gardens, took all the hay and shot one of our cows," wrote one Fauquier resident to his son in September 1862.[59]

When James Marshall, Nathan's landlord, applied for amnesty under President Andrew Johnson's postwar program, he was sixty-three, single and a resident of Fauquier, having moved from Winchester. He wrote that he contributed money and the products of his farm during the war. But now, after it was over, he was in debt, all his personal property had "disappeared," his land was "wasted and dilapidated" and subject to confiscation and he was unable to borrow, he said.[60]

After the war, Nathan had to get his fields in order without the labor of the enslaved people he owned before the war. Records show that a Black family, Lewis and Maria Turner and their three children, were living on the Corder farm in 1870, presumably as paid workers. With this kind of help, Nathan gradually rebuilt his herds and restored his crop production. By 1873, eight years after the end of the war, he was back to where he was at the start. By one estimate, though, it would take another decade for Fauquier residents to rebuild their railroads, schools, stores, churches and homes.[61]

The Corder farm also fell within the Free State, the name given to the roughly twelve-square-mile region in the northwest corner of the county. The Free State was more of a Zion, a mythical place, than a clearly defined one. Legend has it that Lord Fairfax leased tracts in Fauquier to Hessians who came to the United States to fight for the British in the Revolutionary War. Lessees were required to pay rents and taxes and make improvements on their respective grants.

"Little attention was paid, at first, to these mountain tenants who in the lapse of years, had grown into a distinct community," wrote local historian John Gott. "When [later] owners attempted to collect rents in the section, the occupants of the leased farms refused to pay, claiming that the old leases by which they were once bound had now expired, and that they were the rightful owners. After all, had they not cleared the forests, improved the land and built homes and barns?"[62]

According to Gott, Free Staters also developed a reputation as a fierce, combative people whose customs were "at variance with the accepted rules of conduct in other parts of the county." These were men who fought for the mere love of fighting, or as another historian called them, "fist and skull" men.[63]

This tradition of independence and disregard for the law can be seen in the way Nathan and his neighbors dealt with Arthur and Elvira. When Nathan learned of the couple's whereabouts, he did not notify the authorities or simply ignore them and let them live in peace. Instead, he assembled his neighbors, rode north and settled the matter himself. They were the law.

HISTORY OF HATE

The resistance that Arthur and Elvira encountered, the uncompromising prejudice, was not new to Fauquier or Virginia in 1880. The state had long opposed interracial romance between a Black man and white woman and recorded several instances after the Civil War of Black and white love, followed by opposition and flight. The examples illustrate how widespread and deep-seated was this hostility.

In 1870, in the mountains of Highland County, Virginia, a young white woman named Miss Reynolds broke off her engagement to a local white man. Miss Reynolds did not want to marry the man because she was in love with another man, a Black man, who was one of her father's employees.

The *Richmond Dispatch* reported that the unnamed Black man "became desperately in love with [Miss Reynolds], which was mutual, seduced her and on that day eloped with her to parts unknown. Miss Reynolds, we are told, is about eighteen years of age and handsome. The negro is much older, ginger color and homely."[64]

A mob formed, consisting of her family and neighbors and led by her brother. The men believed that the young woman was staying with her lover at his family's home, so they marched on it. Local Black residents learned of the impending attack and greeted the mob with gunfire. Seven white men and two Black men were injured. The young couple was not among the injured; they had fled the area earlier that day.

In reporting on the incident, the newspaper seemed perplexed that an attractive young white woman would run off with a Black man. It concluded that it must have been because her father had been a member of the radical Negro Party, which believed "that a negro is as good as a white man."

In Wythe County, Virginia, in 1871, neighbors went to the home of a local white woman who had been living as the wife of a Black man, described as "black as tar and ugly as a baboon." Their purpose, according to a newspaper account, was to break up the "unnatural alliance." They tarred and feathered the woman and ordered her to leave the neighborhood "at the earliest possible moment." It's not clear what happened to the man.[65]

In Staunton, Virginia, in 1874, a Black man named James Stoneham was fined fifty dollars for illicit cohabitation with a white woman. The woman also was fined, and the couple soon fled the town.[66]

And in 1875, Ben Booker, a Black man, eloped with Mary Davis, an eighteen-year-old white woman from Amelia County, Virginia. They were discovered in Cumberland, about fifteen miles away. According to one news account, "the modern Othello was sent to Amelia to answer for his crime, and the weeping Desdemona left in Farmville to await the coming of her father." Davis was said to be "very pretty" and greatly devoted to her "black, brevet husband."

Later, Booker was sentenced to three years in jail for miscegenation. According to one account, "The girl avowed in court, with unblushing cheek, that she loved Ben better than life and was ready to die for him. (She ought to be sent to the penitentiary with him.)"[67]

As lifelong Virginians, Arthur and Elvira undoubtedly knew of this climate and anticipated how her family would react to their romance, hence the secrecy surrounding it and the surprise when it was revealed. Their story was infrequent but not unheard of in the rural South and was evidence that in Virginia and elsewhere the freedom to love did not apply to all. "The Negro in the Old Dominion whether indentured servant, slave, free person of color or citizen has always been an enormously disadvantaged human being," noted attorney June Purcell Guild.[68]

Virginia's ban against interracial intimacy was more than two hundred years old when Arthur and Elvira began seeing each other. As Judge Leon Higginbotham and Barbara K. Kopytoff noted, "Many people applaud Virginia as the 'mother of presidents' and the 'mother of revolutionaries.' Yet few stress that Colonial Virginia was also the 'mother of American slavery' and a leader in the gradual debasement of blacks."[69]

The prohibitions, aimed primarily at Black men and white women, first appeared in the seventeenth century. Violators were subject to fines, jail time, banishment and corporal punishment. Indentured servants could see

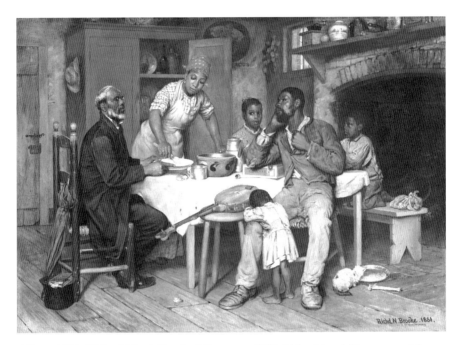

A Pastoral Visit, Richard Norris Brooke, Warrenton, 1881. Using his neighbors as models, Brooke shows African American family life in Jordan's time. *National Gallery of Art.*

their service extended, and any children they bore would also be indentured. Children born to enslaved mothers became enslaved themselves. A white woman who bore a mixed-race child was fined, and if she couldn't pay, church wardens could auction her services for a term of five years. Mixed-race children were bound out until they reached adulthood. A minister who performed a prohibited marriage ceremony also could be sanctioned, as was a preacher in 1870 who performed an interracial marriage in Smyth County, Virginia. He was tried in county court, fined $200 and sentenced to four months in jail.

The language used in these laws—phrases like "abominable mixture," "spurious issue" and "disgrace of the nation"—revealed how white people felt about their Black neighbors. The laws also illustrate the ancient belief that one tribe, community, race or religion was better than another. White residents saw themselves as defenders of their civilization and beneficiaries of a natural order that rated them as superior and privileged and Black people as diminished and subservient.[70]

Francis Fedric, a Black man who was enslaved in Fauquier County in the early 1800s, described how his grandfather argued about religion with his grandmother, saying that slaveholders treated slaves as little more than work animals, and that a slaveholder could sell a slave in the morning and partake of the sacraments in church later that day. "How can Jesus be just, if He will allow such oppression and wrong? How can God be just when He not only permits but sanctions such conduct?" his grandfather asked.[71]

Historian Sheryll Cashin has pointed out that this belief "told whites that they could not marry, sleep with, live near, play checkers with, much less ally politically with a black person." Whiteness was the preferred identity, Cashin added, and the law protected this fictional white purity from mixture. "Over three centuries, our nation was caught in a seemingly endless cycle of political and economic elites using law to separate light and dark people who might love one another," Cashin said.[72]

Chief Justice Earl Warren, writing for a unanimous Supreme Court in the *Loving v. Virginia* case in 1967, which struck down Virginia's ban on interracial marriage, made the same point. Warren reviewed Virginia's long history of racial discrimination and said it was "designed to maintain White Supremacy."[73]

Virginia and the rest of the South were the first to adopt these laws and the last to abandon them. "Penalties for black-white marriage persisted beyond the American Revolution, beyond the Civil War, and indeed, as the Lovings found out, well into the twentieth century," noted historian Peter Wallenstein.[74]

Ironically, Arthur and Elvira might have found Fauquier to be more tolerant had the year been 1860, rather than 1880. Historians such as Martha Hodes have traced a change in southern attitudes toward interracial romances after the Civil War. Before the war, many communities practiced forbearance, though not approval, when a white woman was intimate with a Black man.

"White neighbors judged harshly, gossiped viciously and could completely ostracize the transgressing white woman," Hodes said. "As for the black man, it was a lack of sure violence that is historically significant."[75]

After the war, tolerance became violent intolerance. Elite southern white men, without the structure of slavery, sought to rebuild a society "segregated by race, organized by class and restricted by sex," said Feimster.[76]

"The early years of Reconstruction marked the beginning of an era of terrorism in the American South," Hodes wrote. "Those vanquished patriarchs and their sympathizers replaced slavery with lethal violence in an effort to maintain control over the political, economic and social activities of freed people, including control over the sexual agency of black men and women."[77]

An 1862 drawing of Warrenton looking east toward the courthouse and downtown. *Library of Congress.*

Interracial relationships threatened this new order, and whites reacted with rage. As historian James Kinney has noted, "The prevailing view that no respectable white woman would have anything to do with a black man, that any who did would be driven from society and the black man lynched, seems based on conditions in the South from about 1850 on, rather than the 230 years of slavery prior to that period."[78]

But Arthur and Elvira might have been able to live together unimpeded had they moved northeast to Washington. The nation's capital was in many ways a typical southern city, but its politics were more northern, and it did allow interracial marriages. Of course, Arthur was already married, and Elvira would have known this since he had worked for her father for several years. Yet the couple might have found sanctuary there, more of a live-and-let-live attitude, compared to the hostility they faced in Virginia and Maryland.

The Virginia Supreme Court blessed the notion of white male privilege in 1878, two years before Arthur and Elvira fled. Andrew Kinney, a Black man,

and Mahala Miller, a white woman, had been living together, unmarried, with their three sons in Augusta County. They feared being charged with cohabitation so they traveled to Washington in 1874 to be married, knowing they could not be married in Virginia. However, when they returned home, they were charged with "lewdly associating and cohabiting." Local officials believed that their marriage in Washington was no bar to prosecution, and the court agreed. Finally, on appeal, the Virginia Supreme Court ruled against the couple, with Judge Joseph Christian voicing the racism that had been a ruling principle in Virginia since Colonial times.

"The purity of public morals, the moral and physical development of both races and the highest advancement of our cherished southern civilization all require that they should be kept distinct and separate," Christian wrote. "Connections and alliances so unnatural that God and nature seem to forbid them, should be prohibited by positive law and be subject to no evasion."[79]

To Christian, romance across the color line was unthinkable.

9

SAME OLD RACKET

After the riders kidnapped Jordan in Maryland, it was clear that he would die for what he had done. The only question was when. In Williamsport, the local paper reported that the riders made "threatening remarks" and that "the impression gained ground that the affair would result in a lynching."[80]

Similarly, back home in Fauquier, on the way to the Warrenton jail, the riders stopped briefly in the village of Orlean. One of them predicted that they would never reach Warrenton because "there was a mob in readiness to lynch him." Sure enough, after the group departed Orlean, masked men were spotted riding after them. "Excitement ran high in our village. Bets were made and taken that he would be hung before the hour of midnight," reported the local paper. However, the would-be lynchers never caught the first group of riders before they reached Warrenton and placed Jordan in the county jail.[81]

In Winchester, the local paper reported, "The opinion was very freely expressed that the negro would be lynched before reaching Warrenton, but members of the party assured us they had no such purpose. They are bold and daring fellows, some of whom followed the plume of [Turner] Ashby in the late war, but they are not of the lawless sort."[82]

Actually, they were lawless in all they did. Press accounts described the men as a "posse" and what they did to Jordan as an "arrest." If a posse is an armed band of men summoned by a sheriff to help pursue a criminal, these men were not a posse. They were acting on their own initiative, with no

THE VIRGINIA LYNCHING.

The Quiet Mob that Hanged a Negro for Running Away With a White Girl.

The following despatch from Warrenton, Va., gives the details of the lynching of the negro, Arthur Jordan :

This usually quiet little town was the scene last night of the lynching of a negro under extraordinary circumstances. On the 27th of December last, Arthur Jordan, a copper-colored negro of about forty years of age, who had been employed as a farm hand on the plantation of Nathan Corder, a well-to-do farmer living on the Rappahannock river, in the upper end of the county, eloped with Elvira Corder, twenty-four years old, daughter of the man who had employed him. The negro took the cars at Markham station, and was met by the woman on the train at Salem, fifteen miles further down. The injured father of the girl followed the guilty pair to Washington, and after a fruitless search throught that city and Alexandria, returned broken-hearted to his home. On Saturday last a letter was received by the postmaster at Markham from a gentleman living near Williamsport, Md., saying that there was a negro with his white wife living near him, claiming to be from Markham, and acting in such a manner as to excite his suspicions that all was not right. From the description given the couple were readily recognized as Corder's daughter and Arthur Jordan, and a party of six of the best men in the neighborhood armed and started immediately to Williamsport to capture the latter and bring him back to this county. They were successful in finding him about eight miles above Williamsport, and arrived with him at Markham on Thursday night last. On Friday Justice Lake gave the prisoner a preliminary hearing and, committing him for the action of the grand jury, gave him in charge of a constable and two deputies to carry him to jail at Warrenton, some 20 miles distant, where he arrived the same night and was locked up.

The death of Arthur Jordan attracted attention from dozens of newspapers, including this one from Lancaster, Pennsylvania. *Author's collection.*

69

sheriff or legal sanction. What they did is better described as a kidnapping and, later, as a lynching.

Lynching, or mob murder, was not unheard of in 1880, but it had not become the "sport" that the NAACP would later call it, or "barbarism of a degree of contemptible nastiness unparalleled in human history," as described by W.E.B. Du Bois, one of the group's founders. So many Black people were killed—more than one a week nationwide for more than fifty years—that lynching became what one observer called "one of the most complex and disturbing aspects of the long and rich history of racial violence in the United States."[83]

Lynching was slavery's ugly offspring, said one observer. It occurred in all parts of the United States, but no time or place matched the ferocity of the Old South, the eleven states of the former Confederacy. So many deaths occurred during the "killing years" that patterns developed. It was as if lynching became a ceremony of sacrifice with a familiar format and obligatory rituals. Antilynching crusader Ida Wells-Barnett raged against the practice in 1892, more than a decade after Jordan's death, after learning of lynchings in Arkansas, Alabama, Louisiana and Georgia. They were "the same programme of hanging," she said, "the same old racket."[84]

The most important feature of this "same old racket" was that victims were almost always Black men. White men were lynched during the lynch decades—twenty of them in Virginia between 1866 and 1932. Women, both Black and white, also were victims. But the primary target of these executions—81 percent of those in Virginia—were Black men like Jordan.[85]

Colonel Charles Lynch of Campbell County, Virginia, is said to have originated the practice during the American Revolution as a way of dealing with suspected Tories. Before the Civil War, however, the lynching of Black people was rare because most were enslaved, and slave deaths deprived the owner of property and profit. "The financial investment each slave represented had operated to some degree as a protective shield for blacks accused of crimes," wrote historian Leon Litwack.[86]

After the war, with federal troops eventually removed and home rule restored, the "lynching evil," as Wells-Barnett called it, became a way for whites of every socioeconomic status to retain supremacy over their newly freed neighbors. As one observer said, the closer the Black man got to the ballot box, the more he looked like a rapist. "Southern white men in the post-Reconstruction era reclaimed power, honor, pride and their version of Southern manners with the rope," wrote historian Jacqueline Jones Royster.[87]

TOWANDA, PA., TUESDAY AFTERNOON, J

Great excitement was created at Winchester Va., on Saturday by the unlawful arrest of a colored man who had eloped with a white girl. The lovers were discovered in Williamsport, Md., when a party of white men forced an entrance into the house and after conducting the young lady to a place of safety, bound the negro to a horse, and hastened him across the line into Virginia, with the avowed purpose of lynching him. On reaching Winchester, an officer demanded by what authority they were acting, and on being told they had none, appointed one of them a deputy and allowed them to proceed with their prisoner before a writ of habeus corpus could be procured. The colored population are greatly excited over the exhibition of mob law.

FOR INSURANCE

Busine

A LVORD & S
OB
DAILY REVIEW OFFICE

W OOD & HA
Att
Office corner Main and
JAS. WOOD.

E. H. ANGLE,
OPERATIVE AND M
Office on State street,
office.

B ENTLY MEEH
CLOCK & W
REPAIRER. All at th

D R. T. B. JOHN
PHYSICIAN
Office over H. C Porter
corner Maple and Secon

The Towanda newspaper in Pennsylvania was one of the few that called Jordan's abduction what it was, an "unlawful arrest." *Author's collection.*

Once the Confederacy was defeated, whites grudgingly pledged to accept Black freedom, but they construed it in the narrowest way. "For most it meant only that Black people could no longer be bought and sold," said historian Stephen Ash.[88]

"In all other respects they must remain hewers of wood and drawers of water, condemned now and forever to inferiority and servitude," said Ash. "And whites were ready to use any means necessary, including violence if they could get away with it, to see that their definition of black freedom prevailed in the postwar world."

The earliest listing in the Racial Terror: Lynching in Virginia database is the 1866 death of James Holden, a Black man, in Accomack County.

Eleven Black people were lynched prior to Jordan, and more than eighty followed. Slightly more than half of Virginia's localities experienced a lynching. About a third of them, including Fauquier County, had more than one.[89]

The men who murdered Jordan might have known of a similar case, that of Columbus Miles. Two weeks earlier in Amherst County, Virginia, Miles, a Black man, was accused of an "outrage" against his white employer's daughter. As guards were taking him to jail, a mob of about thirty men overtook them, fired their guns and took the prisoner. The mob carried Miles to a nearby Black church, where they hanged him. His body, "stiff in death," was cut down the following morning. "The general impression seems to be that [his death] was richly merited," reported the local paper.[90]

Nationwide, more than one hundred lynchings of Black people had been recorded by the time of Jordan's murder. More than four thousand followed during the period from Reconstruction to the Great Depression.[91]

The lynching of women—at least 120 killed nationwide during the lynch era—gave lie to the notion that lynching was necessary to protect white women from Black predators. Charlotte Harris was the only Black woman lynched in Virginia. She was accused of inciting a teenager to burn a barn, though the teenager was eventually acquitted. She was hanged from a tree in Rockingham County in 1878.

Peb Falls was the only white woman lynched in Virginia. She was hanged in 1897 in Rockingham County. Falls was not accused of any crime; her infraction seemed to be that she was of "low class," a "disreputable character," and associated with blacks outside of marriage.[92]

As Feimster wrote, "The majority of white female victims of lynching were usually on the fringes of Southern society who were perceived as menaces to their communities." With lynching, white men sought Black deference and white female subordination. Deaths such as Falls's showed how far they would go to punish those who threatened the social and racial order.[93]

Lynchings usually began with allegations of either murder or some sort of sexual contact. The Racial Terror database says that almost half of Virginia lynchings started with an accusation of improper contact, and another 40 percent alleged murder. Stewart E. Tolnay and E.M. Beck reported similar findings across the South in their seminal work, *A Festival of Violence*. However, they reversed the order, with murder cases outnumbering allegations of rape.[94]

The NAACP warned that the crimes alleged against lynch victims were always "pretty loose descriptions" of what actually happened. In Virginia, this can be seen in the allegations of improper sexual contact, which are described as assault, attempted assault, criminal assault, criminal outrage and rape. As historian Edward Ayers said, this "usual crime" sometimes involved rape, "while at other times a mere look or word was enough to justify death."[95]

When Jordan's kidnappers reached Fauquier from Maryland, they took him before a second court official, William Lake, fifty-three, a local farmer who also served as justice of the peace in Markham. Lake deputized a new set of five riders to deliver Jordan to the Warrenton jail.

The actions of the two officials—Crebs in Winchester and Lake in Markham—illustrate official support for this campaign of racial terror. News stories made no mention of any formal charge against Jordan. Several papers described him as a "miscegenist," usually defined as a person who has sex with or marries someone of another race. Others said he had seduced and abducted Elvira. And one said he was guilty of a "social indiscretion." Perhaps everyone understood that a charge against Jordan was an afterthought, that if a Black man was romantically involved with a white woman, he must die.[96]

10

SCRIPTED DRAMA

The NAACP listed community support as one of the defining features of lynching, and this can be seen in Jordan's death. Nathan and his sons did not kill Jordan by themselves, an act of blood revenge. Instead, they sought the help of friends and neighbors.

On the night of Jordan's lynching, at least forty men rode together. These were men like Nathan, farmers, family men, ordinary white men who may have gone to church earlier that day. They were united in retribution for the alleged wrongs done to the Corders.

Their actions assume considerable advance planning. The leaders had to decide on a day and time for the hanging and had to convey that information to the others. The men met at the appointed time and rode together in the darkness from northern Fauquier to Warrenton, about twenty miles. Jordan's death was not a spontaneous act of fury; this was a scripted drama or murder in the first degree.

Still, the men's bravado had its limits. They arrived in darkness, abducted Jordan, killed him and quickly rode away. As one critic observed about lynchers in general, "If they have sufficient justification, why do they sneak out of the responsibility by not only performing the deed in the darkness, but by disappearing afterwards, afraid to take responsibility for their act?" Walter White, executive secretary of the NAACP, would later ridicule lynchers as cowards who were willing to participate in the crime as long as it involved no personal risk.[97]

Jordan's lynching occurred early in the lynching era and offered a preview of what was to come, both in the reason for and the manner in which it occurred. The specifics of his hanging—the method of seizure, the place of death, the size and behavior of the mob, the advance planning and the inevitable conclusion of the coroner's jury—would be repeated many times in the years to come.

Yet his death also defied later categorizations since it was a nighttime murder, not a daylight spectacle, and public rather than private. The lynchers used masks, even though they were well known to one another and to their neighbors.

These self-appointed avengers chose a public place for the lynching, the town cemetery near the jail, rather than a remote wooded site outside town. Other lynchings were done at county courthouses, or on city streets, as was the case in downtown Alexandria, Virginia. In 1893, outside Winchester, Virginia, a mob seized William Shorter on a crowded train and hanged him beside the track in view of all the passengers.

Lynchers left bodies where all could see, as they did with Jordan, since their goals were punishment and intimidation. And in doing so, they did not fear legal sanction or the disapproval of their neighbors.

When Jordan's killers seized him at the county jail, they allegedly deceived jailer Horace Pattie, using a ruse that would be repeated often at other jails throughout Virginia. It began when the men blackened the face of one of their own and tied his hands in front, as if he were a prisoner.

That day, a Sunday in mid-January, had been unseasonably warm, with a high in the fifties. Local papers commented how the springlike temperature seemed to boost church attendance and inspire many to go out walking. By 2:00 a.m. Monday, the streets of Warrenton were dark and deserted and the lights extinguished in most homes. The absence of a bright moon helped hide the crime and those who were about to commit it.

After the men banged on the jail door, Pattie opened it to let them inside. He was once a carpenter and suffered from neuralgia, a painful nerve disorder. Later, a Warrenton resident would write to a Richmond newspaper, complaining that Pattie was "feeble" and implying that he was to blame for the events of that night.[98]

Pattie defended himself to the coroner's jury when it took his testimony the next day. He described how he tried to resist the intruders and how they held him at gunpoint.

The two-story Old Fauquier County Jail was an unusual structure, actually two buildings, an older one and newer one, separated by a narrow

The courtyard between the older portion of the Fauquier History Museum at the Old Jail and the newer cell building. *Author's collection.*

The Fauquier jail comprises two buildings separated by a courtyard. *The Fauquier History Museum at the Old Jail.*

courtyard. The older building, built in 1808, made of brick and facing the courthouse and Waterloo Turnpike, was the original jail, later renovated as a residence for the jailer and his family.

The newer building, directly behind it, held the cells with their heavy metal doors and iron grilles. The building, almost sixty years old and made of fieldstone, had four cells on two floors. The cells were fourteen feet by eighteen feet and housed up to ten prisoners each. Inside, the walls and ceilings were made of wide wood planks, and each cell had a small stove that did little to keep away the cold and damp. Typically, there were three or four prisoners incarcerated there.

Pattie lived at the jail with his wife, Josephine; their five children; and his sixty-five-year-old mother-in-law. One daughter, Josie, died at the jail in the 1870s when she was eleven, and her ghost is said to haunt the building. The jail is now a museum, and the staff there say they have heard her laughing and playing with the office furniture.

That night, the invaders took Pattie's keys and held him prisoner in the courtyard while they entered the cell building to get Jordan. Outside the cell, the passage soon filled with men armed with guns and knives. The only light came from a lantern, held by one of the men.

Pattie could hear one of the men say, "Arthur Jordan?" on entering Jordan's cell.

In his cell, Jordan was awakened by the commotion. He must have known, after all that had happened to him in recent days, that the men were there for him.

The dim light at the cell door made it hard to see, but another inmate, Anthony Smith, in jail that night for fighting, counted maybe eight invaders, all armed and all but two masked. Their leader was unmasked, and another inmate, Frank Matthews, in jail for trying to pawn a pair of stolen boots, described him as stout but not tall, with a full, short beard.

"Keep still and you won't get hurt," the man told Matthews and Smith.[99]

The man ordered Jordan to turn around so he could tie his hands behind his back. He also placed an oak stick in Jordan's mouth to serve as a gag. The stick had a piece of leather at each end, which the man tied behind Jordan's head. The gag was meant to prevent a recurrence of what had happened days earlier in Winchester, when a shackled Jordan screamed for help, attracting unwanted attention. The man also attached a long rope to Jordan's upper arm and led him from the cell. Jordan's hat, coat and boots were on the floor beside his blanket.

"I want my coat," he said.

"We don't care whether you have a coat or not," the man replied.

The man ordered the other inmates to lie down, which they did. "They frightened me," Smith said later.

The men locked the cell door and marched Jordan back to the courtyard. One of them returned the keys to Pattie and told his guards, "Let the old man go."

The men left as they had entered, through the front door. When Pattie got there, he could hear the sound of their retreat in the direction of the Warren Green Hotel stables, south from the jail, on what was then called Seventh Street.

At the front door, Pattie also found his seventeen-year-old son Caldwell, known as Colly, along with Town Sergeant Charles Smith and two town residents, R. Holt and George Maupt. Colly had been asleep in the family apartment but woke when the mob stormed the jail. He realized what was happening and slipped out to raise the alarm.

Colly ran nearby to get Smith, rapped on his door and yelled, "Mr. Smith, they have got the man out of the jail and are going to hang him." Smith said later that he "jumped up quick as I could, slipped my clothes on, ran down the steps and came out at the jail corner." He stopped to

Jordan was forced down what was then South Seventh Street beside the jail and then to the Warrenton Cemetery. *Author's collection.*

listen and could hear commotion a few blocks away in the direction of Charley Payne's grass lot.

"How many of them are there?" Smith asked.

"About sixty," the younger Pattie replied.

"I can't buck against sixty," Smith said. "I'm going to leave them alone."

At the jail, Smith could hear someone in the distance give a low "whoop," a sound he interpreted as a signal, and then the sound of horses moving out of town toward Waterloo Turnpike.

Colly, Holt and Maupt got a lantern and started to go after the men. They asked Smith to join them, but he said no. The riders had probably strapped Jordan to a horse and were heading out of town, he said. The men listened but couldn't hear anything. The town was quiet once again.

"I'm going back to bed," Smith said.

Smith's reaction was perhaps a stark lesson for the young Pattie. Colly had acted decisively in defense of his father and to prevent Jordan's abduction. But Smith, like many Southern officers, made a quick calculation and decided that no Black man was worth risking his life for.

In Lexington, Virginia, in 1869, the jailer on duty when Jesse Edwards was lynched heard the same thing when he went for help. "They advised me to go to bed," he said.

One study of Virginia lynchings found that in up to one-third of the cases, lynchers met with indifference, even cooperation, from local jailers. Pattie said he did offer a measure of resistance when he tried to hide the keys. He was not injured, and the lynchers did not damage the jail, as happened in many later cases.[100]

Critics such as Black newspaper editor John Mitchell of the *Richmond Planet*, writing a decade later, accused jailers of cowardice and complicity during mob murders. Mitchell pointed out that authorities generally did not move their prisoners to distant jails for safety, station extra guards on duty or ask state authorities for help. Jailers surrendered keys or stood aside and let the lynchers take their prisoners. "Very few peace officers defend their prisoners to the point of endangering themselves," said sociologist Arthur F. Raper.[101]

Added Wells-Barnett, "We have reached the unprecedented low level, the awful criminal depravity, of substituting the mob for the court and jury, of giving up the jail keys to the mob whenever they are demanded. We do it in the largest cities and in the country towns."[102]

Meanwhile, the mob pushed and pulled Jordan toward Lee Street, two blocks away. From there, with the outline of what is today called View Top

The mob dragged Jordan from the county jail, down South Seventh Street to Lee Street and finally to the Warrenton Cemetery. *Author's collection.*

Mountain dimly visible in the distance, they headed down the hill to their destination, a few hundred yards away, the Warrenton Cemetery.

Alexander Grandison, a forty-nine-year-old laborer, lived one block from the jail on Eighth Street, with his wife, Betty, forty-seven; his stepdaughter; and a niece. The Grandisons were among Warrenton's 640 Black residents. The Black community already knew the Jordan story—that he had run away with a white woman and been kidnapped—even though he had been in the jail only four days.

The Grandisons were awakened by what they said was a "loud squall." They went to their front door and saw five or six men, one on a white horse, another on a dark horse and the others on foot. Grandison said later that he did not recognize the men in the darkness and heard only two words, "Go on."

"I believe these fellows from up in the country have come and got that fellow and are going to hang him," Grandison told his wife.

By then, Jordan, bound and gagged, must have realized he was being led to his death. He spit the gag from his mouth and twice cried for help. After the second scream, one of the men struck him just above the eye with his rifle butt to silence him. The blow knocked him to the ground unconscious. Someone took the rope that had been on Jordan's arm and placed it around his neck. From there, "willing hands," said one news story, dragged him to the Warrenton Cemetery, five blocks away. His body left an impression in the muddy lane.

At the cemetery, the mob chose a hanging tree in the rear of the property, adjacent to the paling that bounded the property. Other trees could have served as Jordan's scaffold, but by using this one, the men offered symbolic sacrifice at the base of the new Confederate Memorial, a few yards away. One of the county's most prominent landmarks, the white obelisk had been erected three years earlier.

One member of the mob climbed the hanging tree, onto a branch that grew parallel to the ground. He carried the free end of the rope that was around Jordan's neck and dropped it to the men below. They cinched it, launching Jordan's body into the air. Their rope was thin, a plow line. It had already cut deep into Jordan's neck, and now it almost severed his head and made his tongue protrude.

Unlike other lynch mobs, this one did not shoot at the suspended body, an indication perhaps that Jordan was not struggling and was already dead. Instead, the men departed the cemetery, no doubt satisfied with themselves. From their point of view, their plan was straightforward and had worked perfectly. They had ridden into town unchallenged, tricked Pattie and seized the prisoner without firing a shot.

With their actions, the lynchers said they did not trust the judicial system in Fauquier, preferring to administer punishment that was certain, speedy and terrible. For mobs like these, it was not the absence of a criminal justice system that mattered but rather its style. The law was "too capricious, too unpredictable, too formal, too abstract and too concerned with process," said historian Michael J. Pfeifer.[103]

The mob had spared the Corders from testifying in court. Elvira did not have to describe her relationship with Arthur or detail her sexual history. In addition, they had eliminated any chance that Jordan would again walk free. They returned to their homes in northern Fauquier, never to be charged with Jordan's murder.

Right: The Warrenton Cemetery, where Jordan died, looking east toward the county courthouse. *Author's collection.*

Below: The Confederate Memorial in the Warrenton Cemetery is the burial place for Confederate war dead. Jordan was lynched a few feet away. *Author's collection.*

A photo of Warrenton Bar, 1879, shows that Jordan's lynchers couldn't use the absence of judicial system as excuse for his murder. *Fauquier History Museum at the Old Jail.*

With Jordan's death, the lynchers sent one message of fear and vulnerability to African Americans in Fauquier. Their actions sought to deprive Black residents of social, political and economic standing. To the white community, their message was one of solidarity and empowerment. It was also a matter of honor. They would long be able to boast of what they had done. It would become a part of how they saw themselves.[104]

The mob had submitted to the lynching ritual, or perhaps, given the year, helped to define it. In their view, this type of death was a "simple group drama in which evil was defeated, and good was reinstated," said historian Bertram Wyatt-Brown.[105]

From Jordan's point of view, just the opposite was true. The nightmare that began with his sudden abduction in Maryland had ended with his murder in Virginia. He had tried but failed to save himself, and no one else had intervened. His love for a white woman, unremarkable in another time or place, had resulted in his death.

UNLIKELY CHRONICLER

B y morning, town residents had gathered at the cemetery to see the man in the tree. One of the spectators was Dr. Gustavus R.B. Horner, a local physician.

"Before breakfast I was informed of the hanging of a negro last night," Horner recounted in his diary. He lived a few blocks away and went quickly to investigate. He found "several men and boys of all colors looking at the corpse."

With this visit to the cemetery, Horner became an unlikely chronicler of the Jordan saga. He was seventy-five, a white man and retired from the U.S. Navy. There's no evidence that he knew Jordan or had ever heard of him prior to that morning.

A native of Fauquier, Horner attended school in Warrenton and Middleburg and then left Virginia at age eighteen to enter medical school at the University of Pennsylvania. After graduation, President John Quincy Adams appointed him a surgeon's mate, beginning a naval career that took him to Brazil, Uruguay, Portugal, Spain and countless other ports around the world. Later in Horner's career, President Andrew Jackson commissioned him a ship's surgeon.

Horner wrote three medical textbooks, including one devoted to the illnesses and injuries of seamen. He began a diary while on his first sea duty, aboard the frigate *Macedonian*, and continued the practice until the day before he died in 1892. He also collected scientific samples and made sketches of what he saw. His papers include pencil drawings of native plants

Dr. Gustavus R.B. Horner. *From The History of the Blair, Banister, and Braxton Families by Frederick Horner.*

and animals, including the "poisonous mackerel of Gibraltar" and local landmarks, such as the naval hospital at Malta.

After the Civil War, Horner retired and returned to Warrenton, where he lived with his wife, Mary, and their children. It's not clear how Warrenton residents felt about this Yankee in their midst, especially since he served for two years aboard ships that blockaded the Confederate states during the war.

On the morning of Jordan's lynching, Horner again became a reporter, making two sketches of what he saw at the cemetery and describing the scene in his diary. He grabbed a letter someone had sent him and used the envelope with its two-cent stamp still affixed as his sketch pad. He opened the envelope and used the inside for one of his drawings. On the outside, above his name as the recipient, he made what appears to be a practice sketch. With these two drawings and his diary, he created one of the few eyewitness records of Jordan's ordeal.

His practice sketch, perhaps done at the cemetery, includes Jordan's suspended body in a bare tree and, in the background, the Confederate Memorial.

The second sketch, perhaps done later when he returned home, is more detailed and more carefully drawn. Done in pencil, it measures seven inches wide and nine inches long and is now yellow with age. Jordan's body, suspended from one of the leafless branches of a tree, dominates the scene. He is pictured barefoot, in a workman's shirt and pants cinched at the waist, with his hands tied behind him. Horner confirmed news accounts from the time when he drew Jordan with a wound above his right eye, the result of a rifle strike by one of his murderers, and a stick, hanging from his neck attached with leather strips. The stick was shoved in his mouth in the jail, intended as a gag. It proved immediately worthless when Jordan spit it from his mouth on the street outside the jail and cried for help.

Horner's Jordan is a man of medium height and weight, less than six feet tall, who looks older than his twenty-five years. He has a round face with a mustache and close-cropped hair. A caption beside the drawing of the body

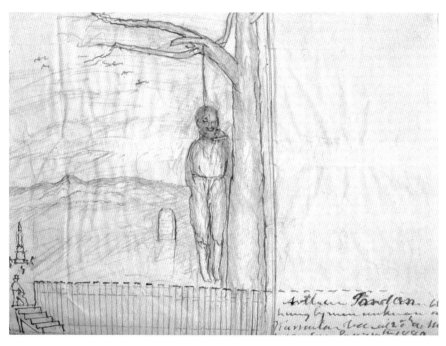

Horner's drawing of the Arthur Jordan lynching. *The Albert and Shirley Small Special Collections Library.*

says, "Arthur Jordan, hung by men unknown at Warrenton, 2 o'clock a.m., Monday, Jan. 19th, 1880."[106]

Horner included several landmarks in his drawing, which today can be used to help identify the location of the hanging. The physician included the Confederate Memorial in the left of the drawing. The monument was built three years earlier and occupies a prominent spot in the cemetery. He also drew the wooden paling, or fence, that formed one of the borders of the cemetery; the stiles, or wooden steps that allowed visitors to climb the fence; and a single tombstone.

Horner pasted the drawing in his diary and wrote a three-page account of the lynching. The diary is one of thirty-three books that he filled with personal observations. He preferred bound books with blank pages, starting a new book when the old one was filled. The first entry in the one he was using at the time of Jordan's death was from 1876. When he filled it later in 1880, it had 231 closely written pages but only one sketch, that of Jordan.

In his diary, recorded after a second visit to the cemetery that night, Horner reported a remarkable development: that the hanging tree was gone,

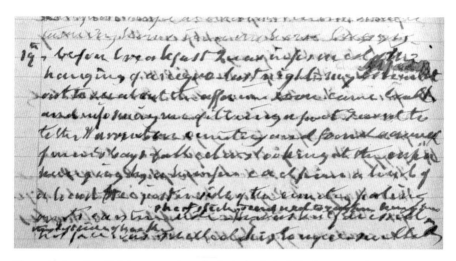

Horner's diary, in which he wrote about Jordan's death, is difficult to read. *Author's collection.*

cut down and removed so completely that "nothing was left to see of its trunk or limbs." He does not say who cut down the tree or why. Perhaps town officials did it, hoping to prevent the tree from becoming some sort of monument. Perhaps Black residents of the town did it in protest and to prevent a recurrence.

Despite this notation, the diary offers less insight into Jordan's murder than the sketches do. One reason is Horner's illegible handwriting. Only snatches of the account can be deciphered. "The pages of the diaries are extremely difficult to read because of the bleed-through of the ink over the years," said one of the archivists at the University of Virginia Library, where the Horner papers are housed.[107]

It would be interesting to learn of Horner's reaction to Jordan's death. The Navy veteran was said to be a private man who avoided alcohol and tobacco and lived a life of Quaker simplicity. Yet here was a mob murder, a summary execution, and not in one of the exotic ports of his travels, but in his hometown at the hands of his neighbors.[108]

Jordan was lowered from the tree at about ten o'clock that morning. His body was taken to the courthouse, next door to the jail, and placed in an empty room. A jury, led by Coroner T.R. Lunsford, heard testimony from several witnesses, including Dr. John Ward, a physician who examined the body.

"From the evidence in the road of his being dragged and the abrasions on his person and clothes, I am of the opinion he came to his death before he reached the tree where his body was found," Ward said. "The evidence of the track of dragging extended a distance of about 500 yards."[109]

Critics of lynching have pointed out that white people eventually became so accepting of lynching that they differentiated between a good lynching (one that featured a quick death) and a bad one (one that featured prolonged agony for the victim, such as burning of the body or removal of body parts). Jordan's death probably would have been among the latter. As one observer said later, it was "a botch[ed] job from beginning to end."[110]

The jurors also heard from Horace Pattie, who described the seizure, and Smith, the town sergeant, who recalled Colly Pattie banging on his door. Town residents Martin and Grandison, who had been awakened from their sleep, described what they saw, as did the inmates who were with Jordan in the cell. One of the inmates, Anthony Smith, a Black man, said he recognized one of the mob members. He told the jurors that he recognized Johnny Ball, a white man, unmasked, in the group of about eight.

"Johnny did nothing but look on," Smith said.

The night before when Pattie returned to the jail cell where Jordan had been to see if the other prisoners were still there, he asked Smith if he recognized any of the mob. Smith said he did not. So the jury decided that his testimony that next day at the hearing "was not entitled to much weight" and dismissed it. Ball lived at the farm of Jaquilin Marshall, one of the riders who abducted Jordan in Maryland. If Smith was correct and Ball was present at the jail, it raises the possibility the men who abducted Jordan in Maryland were among those who murdered him.

The members of the coroner's jury produced a sixteen-page report, describing in detail Jordan's seizure and death. The first paragraph said that the jury's duty was to determine "when, how and by what means" Jordan died. Missing from these instructions was any mention of "who." The jurors made little effort to determine who killed Jordan. If his killers were to be identified and charged, someone else would have to do it.[111]

The jurors concluded that Jordan died by "strangulation with a rope around his neck at the end of which said rope he was dragged, and by which said rope he was suspended by his neck to the limb of a tree." The jurors said he was killed by a mob of forty to sixty men, whose names were unknown to them. They described the night's events as an act of "unlawful violence."

At its meeting the next month, the county board of supervisors approved payments to Dr. Ward for doing the autopsy and to the eight men who served on the coroner's jury. Galloway & Everhart, a local livery stable, received payment for transporting Jordan's body.[112]

In Pattie's jail records, inmates were usually "discharged" at the end of their sentences or transferred to "State Prison." In Jordan's case, the record states simply he was "taken from jail by mob."[113]

The county grand jury met the next month. It interviewed twenty witnesses, white and Black residents from the neighborhood where the Jordans lived. The jurors said they could not determine who murdered Jordan, nor did they blame any county official for what happened. "The enterprise was conducted with such speed and quietness as not to alarm anyone except the jailer and his family," they concluded.[114]

The coroner's verdict and the grand jury verdict would become familiar ones in later years and reveal an official indifference toward lynching and its acceptance as a brutal form of popular justice. As the NAACP concluded, "Coroner's juries repeatedly found that death had come 'at the hands of parties unknown,' a sham verdict, indeed, since lynchers' identities were seldom a secret."[115]

As sociologist Arthur Raper noted, "It is obvious that in most communities where lynching occurs, it is not considered a crime by public opinion or by the courts; state laws against murder, riot, assault and abduction go for naught when lynchers are offenders."[116]

The Black residents of Fauquier were outraged at the brazen lawlessness of the murder but also unable to do much about it. The lynching was a clear

There are several Jordans buried in the Warrenton Cemetery, but it's not clear if any are related to Arthur Jordan. *Author's collection.*

90

warning to them. If there was any doubt about their inferior place in the community and the unacceptability of interracial romance, those doubts were erased. As one news account said, "The colored people are in a high state of excitement and denounce the killing, but of course they will not attempt any rash act."[117]

One imagines that Black residents of the town also may have been upset with Arthur. His affair with Elvira had set in motion a chain of events that put all Black people at risk. When Betty Grandison watched the mob lead Jordan to his death, she said to her husband, "Dress yourself and go out and see what's the matter." He was cautious, however, and replied, "I'm not going out there."

Yet Jordan also showed himself to be bold and fearless, and other Black residents, though frightened by what happened and grieving with his family, may have respected him for it. He had done something that many of them would have been afraid to do. He had followed his heart despite the tyranny of white men's rules.

MURDER EXCUSED

Alone and pregnant in her hotel prison in Maryland, Elvira might have learned of Arthur's fate if she had access to the local newspaper, the *Evening Globe*, and its January 21 story headlined "Lynched."

"Our readers will remember that we last week gave a detailed account of a body of armed men crossing into Maryland from Virginia and carrying off a colored man who had eloped with a white girl," the story said. "At the time it was feared that the negro would be lynched, and the following dispatch from Richmond, under date of Jan. 19, to the Baltimore papers, confirms these fears."

The story said that the mob had invaded Arthur's jail cell in Warrenton at 2:00 a.m., dragged him to the nearby town cemetery and hanged him. "The body was cut down this morning," the paper added. The story made no mention of Elvira, though it concluded, "Jordan's victim is of weak intellect."[118]

When Nathan and his friends abducted Elvira and Arthur, she fought against the kidnapping, fearing that Arthur might be killed. Still, she must have been stunned to learn that it had happened.

One can imagine her grief and pain. For all her careful planning, her determination in the face of obstacles and belief in her abilities, she had judged wrong. We can't know for sure, but she may have expected her family to react fiercely to her departure but didn't care. Perhaps she believed she and Arthur would be safe in another state.

Now she was alone in a strange place and the father of her unborn child had just been murdered. And according to the *Globe* and similar reports, this happened not because of the deadly prejudice of her family and community and not even because of the choices she and Arthur made.

She was not a person of agency, a willing participant in the alliance, according to these accounts. She was a victim. Her romance and flight were not born of her desires or her feelings for Arthur. That was inconceivable. It happened, the accounts said, because she was a simpleton.

The *Globe* story was like many others, as newspaper editors across the country followed the Jordan developments. Many of them found much to admire in the lynchers and described them in heroic terms. The mob consisted of "cool, resolute, determined men," according to one account. Another said, "The remarkable part of this lynching was the entire absence of excitement, the mob proceeding as if in the execution of a solemn duty in avenging the violation of one of the most sacred unwritten laws of society." A third called it "the unlawful execution of a righteous sentence."[119]

One paper headlined its story with "Jordan Jerked." Another said, "He got what he deserved." And a third said, "He will never elope again." As critics have noted, the southern press was creative in providing excuses for the actions of lynch mobs.[120]

One Warrenton resident, using the pseudonym Amateur, wrote to the *Richmond Dispatch*, criticizing the hanging, though he was not concerned for Jordan as an innocent man, a father, husband, brother or son. He feared that the lynching made Warrenton look bad.[121]

The coverage was one measure of the community support that distinguishes lynching from other murders. Jessie Ames, founder of an Atlanta-based antilynching organization of southern white women, said that in communities where lynchings occurred, newspapers considered them painful and regrettable but also excusable, "something in the nature of a terrible cauterization of a poisonous snakebite."[122]

nally adjourned to meet at the Union Hall, at 10 o'clock, to-morrow morning.

Served Him Right.

RICHMOND, VA. Jan. 19—Arthur Jordan, a married negro who had induced a respectable white girl, a daughter of Nathan Corder, to elope with him, but had been caught and lodged in jail at Warrenton, was this morning taken from the jail by a masked party and hanged on a tree in a neighboring cemetery.

Explosion and Loss of Life.

Some newspapers excused Jordan's lynching with headlines such as this one from Mississippi. *Author's collection.*

The *Alexandria Gazette* correspondent, who used the pen name "Chasseur," French for "hunter," ended his news story about Jordan's lynching on a personal note. "I think the lynching was not only justifiable but a necessity," he wrote. "I know of no white man, who, if his daughter or sister was brutally and repeatedly outraged by a negro brute, who taking advantage of her simple mind, frightened her by fear of death into a compliance with his wishes, would not kill him, either by a pistol shot or an appeal to Judge Lynch."[123]

However, other accounts recognized in Jordan's death one of the hypocrisies of southern life, both before and after slavery—how white men were free to rape African American women, but Black men could not touch white women. Wells-Barnett would note this years later when she wrote that white men could rape Black women "without let or hinderance, check or reproof from church, state or press."[124]

The *People's Advocate*, a Black-owned newspaper in Washington, D.C., said that "in no town in Virginia has there been more questionable relations between white men and colored women than Warrenton." The paper recounted one incident when someone posted mock banns of marriage on a church door for several "prominent white men and their colored paramours."[125]

Coverage of Jordan's death was consistent with how he and Elvira had been portrayed earlier. It began with the couple's flight from Fauquier and ended with Jordan's hanging. More than fifty newspapers considered the story newsworthy, including dailies in Australia and New Zealand. Thanks to the telegraph, readers in Pittsburgh, Cincinnati, Baltimore, New York, Richmond, Minneapolis, Washington and St. Louis learned about Jordan's death.

Stories were lengthy and prominently displayed, and they shared a common language, portraying Arthur as a brutish villain and Elvira as his half-witted Dulcinea. In addition, they were graphic and racist, with the use of epithets, the same slurs seen later to describe other lynch victims. In lynching coverage by Virginia newspapers from 1880 to 1900, almost half the stories portrayed Black victims as menacing and primal. Jordan was said to be a "buck fiend" and "sable lover." In jail, he was said to have boasted that "he could serve plenty more white girls as he had served Elvira." And after death, he was said to have gone "where bad darkeys go via hemp."[126]

With a few exceptions, the papers assumed that Arthur was guilty of a crime, though he had not been tried or convicted. None of the stories used the terms *accused* or *alleged* when describing Arthur's actions. Reporters made

LYNCHING A SEDUCER.

A Brutal Negro is Taken From the Jail and Sent Where the Bad Darkeys Go, Via Hemp.

RICHMOND, Va., Jan. 25.—The following account of the lynching of the negro Jordan in Warrenton, Va., for having seduced a half-witted white girl, and afterward eloping with her, is thus described by an eyewitness:

About 2 o'clock in the morning fifty horsemen rode into Warrenton—fifty cool, resolute, determined men, animated by a single purpose. Galloping up the main road, most of them dismounted, and, leaving their horses in care of the few, proceeded on foot to the jail. It was now quite dark; the crescent moon had sunk below the disc, leaving only the light of the stars, that looked coldly down upon the startling scene beneath. A hasty consultation took place, and it was determined to use a ruse to enter the jail. One of their number, who was blacked to avoid identification, had his hands tied before him, and then two men, one on each side of him, walked to the door, the others

CROUCHING IN THE SHADOW,

out of sight. A hurried knock awoke the jailor. Rising from bed he opened the window and inquired:
" Who's there?"
' A prisoner from Rectortown," was the reply.
" Hurry up. We are in a hurry, and want to leave him here."
" All right," said the unsuspecting custodian of crime : " I'll be down in a minute."
Throwing some of his clothes on, he started with a light in his hand and opened the door. There stood the prisoner and guards.
" Wait a minute until I get the keys of the cells," said the jailor, and started up stairs.
A confused noise was heard, and turning round he saw the passage was crowded with men. Instantly he divined the reason, and made a rush for his bedroom. The lynchers were there with him, and forced him to give up the keys, and then warned him to be quiet, backing their words by a significant touch of their revolvers. Going down stairs the regulators went to the large cell, where the object of their search lay on a blanket in front of a stove. There were several other negroes confined for some petty offences. A dim light was burning in the room, shedding a ghastly glare over their scared faces and the masked countenances. Through the *crepe* of the masks there

GLEAMED THE SAVAGE EYES.

" Which is Arthur Jordan ?" asked the leader.
" There he is," answered the frightened, scared prisoners. They made him stand up—wild, dazed, too frightened to speak, he stood shivering, while his hands were tied behind him—then a piece of green oak, a foot long and two inches in diameter, about the size of an iron car-coupler, was placed between his teeth, and he was led out, the party locking the door behind them. Reaching the cutward door, they placed a rope around his neck, and started down the back street that leads to the Warren Green Hotel stables. Hardly had they reached the lane that turns at right angles from the stables, and runs to the Warrenton Cemetery, distant about two hundred and fifty yards when the gag came out of the prisoner's mouth, and he shouted out twice very loudly. It does not need a clairvoyant to tell what followed.
The lane from the stables to the churchyard is very muddy, and as he shouted, a heavy instrument, probably the butt of a pistol.

Many newspaper stories used racial epithets in describing Jordan and other lynch victims. *Author's collection.*

no attempt to learn the identity of the men who killed him. To many, Jordan's death was inevitable and appropriate.

Similarly, the use of phrases like "exceedingly pretty" to describe Elvira and "by no means prepossessing" to describe Arthur sent a message to readers. "Men are stirred," said Ames, when a beautiful woman is taken advantage of by a Black man. "No one with a drop of red blood in his veins will stand back."[127]

As for Arthur, editors downplayed his appearance, as if to say he was not unusually gifted or handsome, and because of that, was not the kind of lover that a white man would envy. In these and other ways, coverage in white-owned papers excused and encouraged lynching.

Criticism did appear in several places, including the *People's Advocate*. "All honor" to R.G.L. Paige, a Black member of the House of Delegates, for demanding that the Virginia governor get involved, the paper said.[128] A Lebanon, Pennsylvania paper asked Maryland governor William Hamilton to extradite those responsible for Jordan's kidnapping. And in Harrisburg, Pennsylvania, the paper criticized the Virginia legislature, saying its inaction was an endorsement of lynching.[129]

Later critics, such as Wells-Barnett and Mitchell in his *Richmond Planet*, began to "howl loudly" at the anarchy of lynching. They called on local and state officials to do their duty and protect Black residents. To them, lynch victims were human souls made in God's image with a right to life. Lynching violated their constitutional guarantees, such as the presumption

A COLORED MISCEGENATIONIST LYNCHED BY A VIRGINIA MOB.—It was briefly mentioned in yesterday's STAR that Arthur Jordan, a colored man, who was placed in jail at Warrenton, Va. a few days ago, charged with the seduction and abduction of Elvira, a white girl, the daughter of Mr. Nathan Corder, living near Markham station, Fauquier county, Va., was taken by a mob from the jail on Monday morning, between the hours of 1 and 2 o'clock, and hung. The mob numbered from 40 to 60, and gained access to the jail by making Horace Pattle, the jailer, believe they wished to commit a prisoner, who seemed to be a black man. The jailer's suspicions being aroused he fled to his room, but was followed and made to surrender the keys of Jordan's cell. Jordan's hands were tied behind him, a gag put in his mouth, and a rope placed around his neck. He was then dragged to the cemetery, about two hundred yards from the jail, and hung to a locust tree. The physicians think he died of strangulation before he was hung on the tree. Jordan had lived with Nathan Corder for two years. Miss Corder, his victim, was a half-witted girl, but rather attractive in personal appearance. The coroner's jury returned their verdict that Jordan came to his death at the hands of parties unknown, except one Johnny Ball, whom Anthony Smith, a colored prisoner in jail, claims to have recognized. But little credence is attached to Smith's declaration, as he stated to several parties that he did not know any of the men who entered the jail.

Above: The most frequent charge against Jordan, though never a formal one, was miscegenation, as seen here in a Washington newspaper. *Author's collection.*

Right: Newspapers, including the *Washington Post*, excused lynching and assumed the victim was guilty as accused. *Author's collection.*

LYNCHED BY A MOB.

A NEGRO FIEND IN VIRGINIA HANGED TO A TREE.

The Crime for Which He Suffered—Quiet Movement of the Lynchers, Who Are Masked and on Horseback—Description of the Dead Man.

Special Dispatch to THE POST.

WARRENTON, Va., Jan. 19.—Near the little village of Markham, a station on the Manasses Gap railroad, in Fauquier county, there lives a respectable, hard-working family named Corder, consisting of an old man, his wife, two sons and a daughter. They are honest and industrious and bear the best of reputations. The daughter is a fine-looking buxom girl, but very simple in her intellect. A negro man named Arthur Jordan has been employed by the Corders for three years. He was about thirty years old and has a wife and two children. It seems that last summer he violated the girl and threatened to kill her if she informed her family of the fact, and by the same threats he made her submit to his wishes during the late summer and fall. Some days ago Miss Corder became *enceinte*, and the negro fearing detection, persuaded the unfortunate girl to run off with him. Together they fled and were pursued by the Corders, assisted by some neighbors, and were overtaken in Maryland. The girl, because of her condition, was left in Maryland and the negro was brought here and lodged in jail last Wednesday. There was no feeling in this town on the matter, but a tempest was brewing in the vicinity of the Corders' home. This morning at 2 o'clock the jailor was awakened by two men purposing to bring a prisoner. By this means they induced him to open the doors and soon secured the keys of the prisoner's cell. Arthur Jordan was then aroused from his slumber, his hands tied behind him, a wooden gag placed in his mouth, a rope tied around his neck. He was then led towards the graveyard, some three hundred yards distant. A few steps from the jail he managed to get the gag from his mouth and shouted two or three times. He was then knocked down and dragged through the mud to the cemetery, the rope attached to his neck and hung from the branches of a small locust tree. He was evidently unconscious, if not dead, when hung. The lynchers consisted of some fifty horsemen, blacked and with masks on. The coroner's jury found a verdict of death by hanging, but criminated no one. There is terrible excitement among the colored people here, but nothing will come of it. This is the first case of lynching that has happened here. Public opinion in the country justifies the act. Arthur Jordan was a large bull-necked, thick-lipped negro, very black and forbidding-looking. He little expected the fate in store for him, was very defiant, and boasted but yesterday that he would soon marry other white women as he did Miss Corder.

96

of innocence and the right to a fair trial. It also hurt the community, they argued, by driving capital and prosperity from the door.

The *Religious Herald*, a Richmond, Virginia weekly, offered what would become a common type of editorial on lynching, cynically described as the "two-handed" approach, with a prominent "however" or "but" midparagraph to temper the criticism. On the one hand, the paper said, nobody opposed the mixing of the races more than it did. On the other hand, Jordan's death was inexcusable, the paper said. "A public building is entered fraudulently," it said, "the custodian is overpowered, and a man, innocent in the eyes and judgment of the law, is seized, gagged and ferociously murdered."[130]

Even though it was murder they were commenting on, editorial writers couldn't bring themselves to voice full-throated criticism. They wavered, often defending the mob's action as justifiable homicide, citing delays in court procedure or the uncertainty of punishment. They tempered their criticism in solidarity with the notion of white supremacy. What happened to Jordan was terrible but understandable given his crimes, editorials said. One would expect a father to chase after the couple and bring them home, but what happened after that was regrettable.

In this way, newspapers did not lead their communities. They feared being out of step with their readers and followed rather than challenge them. They excused what was obviously felonious behavior. It would be decades before white-owned papers would muster any serious opposition to lynching. Added Ames, "The [papers] find themselves in the difficult position of a rider who must sit two horses at the same time, one facing backward, the other forward."[131]

The *Weekly Louisianian* in New Orleans adopted this approach, finding merit and misconduct in the lynching. In a front-page editorial, the paper said it understood how an angry people might resort to lynching when the alleged crime is "particularly odious."

But Elvira was an adult and could do as she pleased, it said. "Miss Elvira knew perfectly well what she was doing and had no other counsel in the matter but the dictations of her own mind and heart. If Jordan is guilty of any offense, it is that of having deserted his family to go off with another woman."

Even so, given Nathan Corder's standing in the community, no one would fault him for ignoring the law and rashly chasing after the couple, the paper said. Unfortunately, it didn't end there, the paper added. A man was killed even though Elvira was not a minor, and there was no hint of violence on Arthur's part.[132]

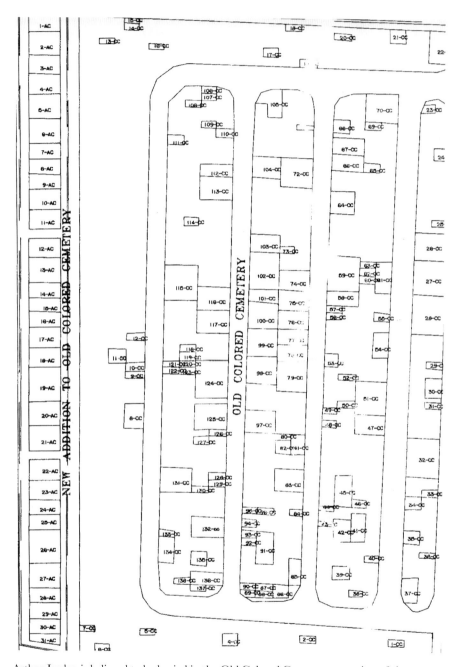

Arthur Jordan is believed to be buried in the Old Colored Cemetery, a portion of the Warrenton Cemetery. *Author's collection.*

The *Alexandria Gazette* flirted with condemnation but also stopped short, recognizing that if Elvira was an "imbecile," Jordan's murder was understandable. However, added the paper, "it would have been infinitely better to have allowed the law, which had the culprit in its hands, to have meted out to him the prescribed punishment."[133]

After the coroner's inquest, Jordan was buried in the "colored cemetery," presumably the Black section of the Warrenton Cemetery. Other residents named Jordan are buried there, but it's not clear if they are related to Arthur. His grave, if there, is unmarked.

Years later, Wells-Barnett attended a speech by Mitchell and heard him read the names of lynching victims. "They had no requiem, save the night wind, no memorial service to bemoan their sad and horrible fate," she wrote. "Their bodies lie in many an unknown and unhonored spot."[134]

13

TURN MY BACK, SHUT MY EYES

The Virginia House of Delegates was in session in Richmond when Jordan was murdered, and the members took up the case two days after his death.

A Black delegate from Norfolk, Richard G.L. Paige, pointed out that Jordan died two weeks after the lynching of another Black man, Columbus Miles, in Amherst County. Paige feared that other "sons of the Sahara," as he called them, would soon be murdered, which proved prophetic. "Within the present month, acts of lawlessness and violence have been perpetrated by mobs upon innocent citizens of this state, resulting in brutal murders by lynching of two colored persons," he said. Paige wanted Governor Frederick Holliday to post a suitable reward for the capture of the persons responsible and to bring them to trial.[135]

Paige said both deaths occurred without any proof that the two men had violated the law and in localities where local officials could have brought them to trial if evidence existed. He described Miles's actions toward a white woman as "indecencies," and he said Jordan had simply "taken a walk" with a white woman.

"The question is whether or not an armed mob can take without any signs of justice and hang the citizens of this Commonwealth, be they black or white," he said.[136]

Paige was born a slave in Norfolk. After being freed, he moved to Boston, where he trained as a machinist. He returned to Virginia after the Civil War

The old House of Delegates chamber at the Virginia State Capitol. The debate between Paige and Payne about Jordan's lynching took place here. *Author's collection.*

and studied law at Howard University. He was a successful attorney with substantial real estate holdings and one of the early leaders of the college that became Hampton University.[137]

He was serving his third term in the Reconstruction-era assembly and, at age thirty-three, had apparently decided that freedom was won, not given. He threatened to sue a Richmond theater when it refused him admittance, and he probably angered fellow legislators when he accused them of hypocrisy. He pointed out that they objected to a Black-white romance such as Arthur and Elvira's, yet they had consorted with their Black servants and slaves and had created a race of bastards. "A man that is acquainted with Richmond as well as I am and acquainted with the actions of some of my white brethren before me, can afford to say it is wrong," he said.[138]

Paige's frankness was met by an equally harsh response from one of the white legislators, William Henry Fitzhugh Payne, a lawyer from Fauquier. Their standoff in the House that day was brief but served as a mirror on the state of race relations in Virginia in 1880 and a preview of the chaos that was to come.

LEGISLATURE OF VIRGINIA,
SESSION 1871 and '72.

Above: Delegate Richard G.L. Paige (*bottom row, fifth from right*). *Encyclopedia Virginia.*

Right: General William H.F. Payne. *Virginia Museum of History and Culture.*

Both Paige and Payne were natives of the state and men of struggle and achievement. One was young, Black and unafraid to test the limits of the new freedoms. The other was white, almost fifty and longing for a lost order.

Payne was new to the assembly, serving his first term, but the other delegates had no doubt heard about him. Payne's family had helped settle the colony, and he could claim a grandfather who commanded troops at Yorktown during the Revolutionary War. He was a graduate of the Virginia Military Institute and the law school at the University of Virginia, and he was the former commonwealth's attorney in Fauquier. Yet it was his service with the Confederate army during the Civil War that was most often talked about. To his colleagues in the assembly and to everyone else, he was known as General Payne.

Payne helped organize the sons of the planters in Fauquier into the feared Black Horse Cavalry. He served from the earliest days of the conflict until its end. He fought in several major battles, including Williamsburg, Brandy Station, Gettysburg, Wilderness, Spotsylvania Courthouse, Cold Harbor and Manassas, rising to the rank of brigadier general. He was wounded multiple times, including a near-fatal injury when shot in the face at Williamsburg. "I was left between the lines and almost drowning in my own blood," he wrote.[139]

He was captured several times, detained in prison and then exchanged for Union prisoners. After the South's surrender and one day after Lincoln's assassination, he was arrested, taken to Washington and marched through the streets to prison, on the suspicion that he had something to do with Lincoln's murder. "Hang them," he recalled the crowds yelling. Soon it was determined that another man named Payne was involved, and this Payne was freed. Later, in 1865, after the war's end, when Payne asked President Andrew Johnson for a pardon, Payne said the war had "stripped me of every vestige of property and has left me maimed in body with a wife and seven children dependent upon me."[140]

That day in the General Assembly, Payne defended the mob's murder of Jordan, describing him as a married man who had seduced a naive young white woman. "He was in the employment of the father, and using his power and position in the house, he seduced this idiotic child and carried her out of the state as his mistress," Payne said.

Payne added that Elvira shouldn't be expected to testify "before a gaping crowd." He then spoke for many white southerners when in a single sentence he offered a defense of lynching and denunciation of his Black neighbors. His words, spoken from the floor of the state capitol by an elected member

eterans of the Black Horse Troop gathered in the garden behind Gen. Payne's house on May 20, 1890, before oing to Richmond for the dedication of the statue of Robert E. Lee. Attendees are identified in silhouette below.

An 1890 reunion picture of General William H.F. Payne (*first row, third from left*) and the Black Horse Cavalry. *The Fauquier History Museum at the Old Jail.*

of the assembly, may not have surprised the Black legislators seated around him or the Black residents of the state, but they must have discouraged them. If they had any hope of equal rights under the law in a new postwar Virginia, they now had to temper that hope.

"When such [a] thing as this happens," Payne said, "I will turn my back and shut my eyes for a few minutes while the operations are going on."[141]

The assembly applauded, and Payne asked that Paige's motion be sent to committee for study. The vote was 69–13, with all of the Black delegates opposing it and all but one of the white delegates supporting it. Colonel Robert Stribling, who had been incorrectly named a member of the group that abducted Jordan in Maryland, supported the motion.[142]

The *Wilmington (DE) Daily Gazette* endorsed Paige's proposal and predicted in an editorial that a legislative committee would travel to Warrenton to learn what happened; that Maryland authorities would extradite the men who kidnapped Jordan; and that the people who lynched him would be arrested, tried and punished. None of that happened. There was no investigation, no extradition, no punishment. Payne's motion effectively killed Paige's proposal.[143]

In the coming months and years, as the number of lynchings grew, others joined Paige to denounce the practice as contrary to the laws of God and

Visitors still show support by leaving tokens, coins and flags on the grave of Colonel John S. Mosby in the Warrenton Cemetery. *Author's collection.*

man and to call on state and local authorities to do their duty and protect Black people. Their cries went unheeded.

After the war, in his request for a presidential pardon, Payne wrote, "I gave my heart entirely to what I honestly believed to be the service of my country, and I claim that in this loyalty, mistaken though it may be, the U.S. Government will find the best element for valuable citizenship."[144]

However, Payne's pledge of valuable citizenship can be questioned. In 1903, when asked to reflect on his war years, he sounded much as he did that day in the House of Delegates. "I am as true a Confederate today as I was when I marched from Warrenton to Manassas," he wrote. "I have never ceased to regret the loss of our cause. I think that the greatest calamity that has ever befallen the country is the wreck of the Confederacy."[145]

14

NO TRACE OF ELVIRA

When Shawn Nicholls and I pulled into the driveway at Darryl Jenkins's home, he was waiting for us at the kitchen door.

"I've been looking forward to this," he said.[146]

I had arranged to meet Darryl and his wife, Arlene, at their home in central Fauquier County. Shawn, a skilled researcher and resident of Fauquier, had been helping me uncover the story of Arthur and Elvira. The Jenkinses were anxious to hear about our work, and we wanted to learn about a project they were working on. Perhaps they could help us find Elvira Corder.

Darryl and his wife are in their seventies, gray-haired and fit. He is a drone expert, still working full time in the aerospace industry. "We have to pay the mortgage," joked Arlene, a retired lobbyist. The two also have become self-taught experts on the Fauquier Poorhouse. Talking to them about their work requires full attention, as they speak enthusiastically and finish each other's sentences.

The couple once gave a talk about the poorhouse to a standing-room-only audience at the Fauquier Heritage and Preservation Foundation in Marshall. Since then, families have contacted them to talk about distant relatives who lived at the poorhouse or, as Shawn and I did, to see if they could help find someone lost to history.

What started as a fun, part-time hobby for the couple, digging through old county records, has become something more. Darryl said he and Arlene have been surprised at how emotional people are when recalling their ancestors. He hopes that their research helps preserve these memories, in addition to

Darryl Jenkins at the site of the Fauquier County Poorhouse cemetery. *Author's collection.*

showing how one rural Virginia county in the nineteenth and early twentieth centuries cared for its poor.

Fauquier's poorhouse could be better described as a poor farm, set on rocky, hilly acreage on what the county now calls Poorhouse Road. The house itself has been renovated by its current owner but once housed up to thirty people on two floors in big dormitory-style rooms. Able-bodied residents worked on the farm or were hired out to work for neighbors. The Fauquier poorhouse was one of many in the United States, and as one account described them, "Rules were strict and accommodations minimal."

The Anglican Church was the first to operate a poorhouse in Fauquier, as early as 1820. The county assumed operation in 1874 and ran the home at public expense until 1927, Darryl said.

The poorhouse was seen as a stepping stone to the grave, a holding place for the old and infirm who had no family. Residents were usually poor and disabled or unable to care for themselves. In 1880, for example, the federal census counted nineteen people living in the home. Mariah Coles was described as "blind and crippled." Molly Ryan was said to be "idiotic." M. Woodson was there because his feet had been frostbitten.[147]

The Jenkinses have compiled two master lists with dozens of names, one of poorhouse residents and the other of those buried in the poorhouse cemetery, on a hill overlooking the home.

"She's not here," said Arlene, after searching both lists for the name of Elvira Corder.

Arlene's words were frustrating but not surprising. Shawn and I had experienced many similar moments in our search for Elvira. We had traced her from her birth in Fauquier in 1855. We could see her in census records, living with her mother, father and brothers. We saw how her mother and baby sister died, how her father remarried and her stepmother and her two children moved into the family home. We learned of her limited schooling and her farm life.

Finally, in press accounts, we read of her fateful romance with Arthur Jordan, her pregnancy and flight with him to Maryland, her family's pursuit, Arthur's murder and her confinement in a Williamsport, Maryland hotel.

One of the last mentions of her in any public record was in January 1880, when news reports said that the Corder family intended to return to the hotel for her and travel home by train because of her "delicate" condition. There is no evidence that this ever happened.

Arlene Jenkins's search of poorhouse records bolstered our theory that Nathan did not retrieve his daughter in Maryland. His fury and embarrassment must have been immeasurable, given all that happened after her flight with Arthur. It's hard to imagine Elvira, pregnant with a mixed-race child, returning to Fauquier to live at the family farm or a few miles away at the poorhouse, a constant reminder of what she had done.

In this way, our visit to the Jenkinses was disappointingly familiar. We had traveled to many other locations in Maryland and Virginia, talking to local historians and searching records. Each visit began with a spark of hope, a faint notion that this time would be different, that we would be able to solve the mystery of Elvira. Yet each visit, every search, ended in frustration.

For example:

- Washington County, Maryland, where Elvira and Arthur lived, had its own poorhouses, called the Belleview Asylum and the Alms House. Would Elvira, a pregnant stranger, have moved from the hotel to one of these homes? Admissions and cemetery records do not mention her. In fact, Maryland counties did not begin to collect death records for almost another decade.
- Many years before Elvira's birth, several of Nathan's relatives joined a wagon train and sought a better life by moving from Virginia to Missouri. Had Nathan sent his daughter to Missouri to live with one of her relatives? Or perhaps with her mother's

family in Rappahannock County, Virginia? Census records make no mention of her in either place.

- By 1905, more than twenty years after Elvira's disappearance, three orphaned children moved in with Elvira's brother, Will, and his wife, Alice, who was the children's aunt. One of those children was Frances H. Reid, who grew up to be the longtime editor of the *Loudoun Times-Mirror* newspaper in Leesburg, Virginia, and president of the Loudoun Historical Society. Had Reid learned of the story of Elvira and Arthur and recorded it somewhere? Her papers at the Balch Library in Leesburg make no mention of it.
- When Arthur and Elvira arrived in Maryland, they lived and worked at the Shupp farm. Had Elvira moved from the hotel to live again with one of the Shupps? Census records make no mention of her there—or anywhere, for that matter.
- If, at some point, Elvira realized that her family did not intend to return to Williamsport for her, she might have moved to Baltimore, a bigger city that offered anonymity and opportunities for a single woman and mother of a mixed-race child. But her name does not appear in Baltimore records, which are more extensive than those of other Maryland localities. Nor is her name found in the courthouse in Hagerstown, the Washington County seat, in its birth, adoption, guardianship or marriage records.
- A search of newspaper archives revealed an intense interest in the story of Elvira and Arthur. Reporters offered intimate details about Arthur's death, including his abduction from the jail and the type of tree chosen for his hanging. Yet no one was curious about Elvira.

So what did happen to her? And what of her child, presumably born in mid-1880?

Her disappearance is a point of weakness in the story but also a reason for doing it. It was as if she was erased, stowed in a hotel in Maryland, abandoned and never heard from again. In the absence of reliable records, we answer questions about her as possibilities, built on what we know of her, her family and the world in which they lived.

Confined to the hotel, Elvira was no doubt traumatized by what had just happened. She had just watched Arthur be led away in shackles, and now she was alone in a strange place. Desperation in the face of these overwhelming forces would be understandable. We have no evidence that Elvira aborted her baby or abandoned it. But the archives of Washington County, Maryland, tell of other young women, living at the same time, in the same locale, faced with similar strains, who reacted in shocking ways.

In October of that year, someone found a baby—a white female—floating in the Potomac River near the second pier of the Harper's Ferry Bridge in the southern part of the county. When Dr. B.B. Ranson, the coroner, examined the body, he concluded that the child was about two months premature and was apparently dead before being thrown in the river. He reported that the afterbirth was still attached, and he found no visible marks or signs of violence. The mother, perhaps a young, single woman like Elvira, chose to abandon her daughter rather than face an uncertain future.[148]

A few months later, authorities were summoned to a home in Boonsboro in the southern part of the county, where they found the body of Susan Shriver, a single white woman. The coroner listed the cause of Shriver's death as an abortion and subsequent exposure. The abortion was performed "either by herself or through the assistance of others unknown," he concluded. Apparently, Shriver was driven to terminate her pregnancy by her own hand or, if she had help, by that of someone who abandoned her to die.[149]

And in January 1886, the coroner was summoned to a home in Edgemont, in the eastern part of the county, where he found a just-born baby who had died of exposure in the winter cold.

County records, though spare, tell a sad story of a troubled woman named Elizabeth Ridenour. Elizabeth's brother, Daniel Ridenour, said that Elizabeth's behavior was unusual that morning. She was restless and went in and out of the house several times. Daniel's wife concluded that Elizabeth must be ready to deliver her baby and told her husband to go for the midwife.

When he returned with Mrs. Nole, the midwife, Elizabeth had already delivered the infant and was in bed. However, the baby was not to be found. Daniel and his wife went outside to search for it, while Mrs. Nole confronted Elizabeth.

"Tell me what you've done with it," Mrs. Nole said.

Elizabeth resisted at first but eventually told Mrs. Nole that she didn't know what to do with the baby, so she hid it in the dog house.

Mrs. Nole went outside to find Daniel and his wife. "It's in the dog house," she told them.

Mrs. Nole carried the infant back to the house and tried to revive it by immersing it in a tub of warm water, rubbing it and warming it beside the stove. Nothing worked. She told the coroner's inquest that the child had been outside in the weather for maybe ninety minutes and could not be saved.

When Dr. C.A. Baldwin interviewed Elizabeth, she told him that she gave birth on the porch. She said she was standing when she delivered the child, and that the baby cried when born. County records don't indicate if the child was a boy or girl. Baldwin could find no evidence of violence, only a spot on the baby's knee, which probably happened when the child fell to the floor. The "naval string" was ruptured, also evidence of the fall, Baldwin said.

The jurors concluded that the baby died because of Elizabeth's neglect, but they also said that she was "irrational" or of "unsound mind" and was not responsible. "Her mind is very much impaired," they said.[150]

There is no evidence that Elvira acted as these women did. But, like them, she was pregnant in a world that offered little support. She must have experienced similar uncertainty and stress and shared in their lonely desperation.

But we also see in Elvira a belief in her abilities, a resistance to what was expected of her. We can imagine that she thought, as Arthur did, that she had done nothing wrong. She no doubt blamed others and with good cause, since the prevailing hatred, the racial prejudice common to her time, prevented the couple from living in peace.

Even so, she must have had moments of regret. Her choices, from her decision to welcome Arthur as her lover to her decision to run away with him, had proved disastrous. Perhaps she should have anticipated what would happen. She knew her family and neighbors well.

In the hotel, Elvira may have been frozen in inaction, disoriented by shock and grief, passively awaiting the return of her father. Yet it is also possible that she was an actor rather than one who is acted on. Did she immediately plan her escape and future? And what if her family never returned for her? How long would it take her to realize this?

She had much to consider. She had to plan for the delivery of the baby, where to live after the birth and how to support herself and her child. She was not without skills. As the oldest, she had cared for her younger brothers and helped with the farm and household chores, especially after her mother's death. Fantine in *Les Misérables*, facing a similar dilemma, turned to prostitution.

Elvira may have been resigned to the fact that she would never go home again, even indifferent to her own survival. Yet now she had a child to think about. She would soon be a mother. She would have been aware that she had to endure if her baby was to survive. Under this scenario, she had to rouse herself and continue her fight, this time not with her lover but with her baby.

One possibility—the fate mentioned most often in press coverage—can be dismissed. News accounts stated that the Corders planned to go back to the hotel and return with her to Fauquier. Yet there is no indication that Elvira ever again resided in Fauquier and, given the circumstances, little chance of it. Her actions were so outside the social norms of 1880 rural Virginia, and her family so rigid about those norms, that it is unlikely they would bring her home.

When Emily, in *David Copperfield*, runs away with Steerforth, her uncle Dan vows to bring her home. "Dan, there's nothing you can do now," says Clara, his sister. "You know what she'll become when he's finished with her. She's lost."[151]

Perhaps then the Corders sent word to Maryland that they would not be returning for their daughter, that they had decided to abandon her. Or perhaps Elvira did not await word from her family but decided to save herself and her unborn child by fleeing her confinement, changing her name and beginning a new life elsewhere.

Another possibility is murder. In this scenario, the Corders returned to Maryland after Jordan's lynching, plucked Elvira from the hotel and killed her—an honor killing. It may seem unlikely that a father would kill his eldest child and only daughter. Yet Nathan had already acted as a man seeking retribution for a grievous injury. Only days earlier, he had plotted the kidnapping and murder of Elvira's lover. And when pursuing the couple in Alexandria, soon after their flight, he told a policeman, "I promised her mother that I would bring her back dead or alive."

Murder also would explain the disappearance of Elvira from the public record. It is possible to trace the arc of her family's history for another forty years, to mark the deaths of Nathan and Elizabeth, the marriages of her brothers and the births of their children, the sale of the family farm, the relocation of John and Will and their families to neighboring Loudoun County and finally their deaths and burials.

It's also possible to trace Anna Jordan's brief life after her husband's death, her remarriage and her death from consumption in Warrenton. Yet exhaustive searches return not a word about Elvira. No mention of an address, birth, adoption, marriage or death. No tombstone marks her burial. She was erased without a trace, as if she had never existed. Perhaps this was exactly as her father intended. Perhaps the Corders did not want Elvira to be heard.

The last mention we have of Elvira in any public record is a cryptic paragraph in her father's will, written in 1890, ten years after she fled. In the first part of the document, he makes an equal division of his holdings among his wife and sons.

He mentions Elvira in paragraph four, almost as an afterthought, as if his attorney insisted on it. He says simply that she died in Maryland. He does not explain when she died, where she died or how. His words, however, made clear that Elvira died far from home, sometime between 1880, when she fled with Arthur, and 1890, when he wrote the will. His words also made clear that he may have tried to forget what happened, but he had not forgiven.

He wrote: "This is to certify that I have not overlooked my daughter Elvira Corder who died in the State of Maryland and to whom and to her issue should she have left any, I give and grant them one cent as their sole interest in my estate."

It is interesting to consider what Nathan meant when referring to Elvira's death. It is probable that she did die. But it is also possible that Nathan disowned her, that she died a social death, because of the dishonor she brought to him and his family.

What seems certain, however, was Nathan's anger. As Capulet tells his daughter in *Romeo and Juliet*, "What is mine shall never do thee good."[152]

With this rage, Nathan also confirms the voluntary romance between his daughter and Arthur and refutes any possibility that she was coerced. Ten years after her flight, Nathan was still angry and chose again to punish her and her child. In one sentence, he both recognized her and her "issue" and protected himself and his heirs from them. He owned a home and three hundred acres of prime farmland, yet Elvira and her child were left only a hostile token: a penny.[153]

EPILOGUE

Nathan Corder died two years after writing his will, in January 1892, at the age of seventy-three. He is buried beside his wife, brother and sister in an overgrown private cemetery in Rappahannock County.

Nathan's death and the terms of his will revealed what appears to be tensions within the family, especially between John and Will, his two oldest sons, and Elizabeth, their stepmother.

The two brothers immediately turned to the local court to settle issues that many families are able to work out on their own. Their filings also raised anew the question of their sister Elvira, who fled the home years earlier to live with Arthur Jordan. Was she driven away, at least in part, by an unhappy home?

In February, one month after Nathan's death, John, thirty-four, and Will, thirty-two, asked the Fauquier County Circuit Court to appoint commissioners to appraise and sell the family's personal property. (Their brother, Charles Corder, was nineteen at the time and still a minor.) It's not clear why the brothers took this step. One possibility is that the sale was done as a way of converting the family's possessions into cash to pay debts or divide the proceeds among the heirs. But it meant that many of the items in the home—from the beds that family members slept on to the chairs they sat on—would be offered at public auction. If someone in the family wanted to retain an item, he or she would have to outbid other interested buyers.

The next month, three court-appointed commissioners visited Wheatfields, the Corder farm near Hume in northern Fauquier. The trio went from room

Nathan Corder's tombstone in Rappahannock County, Virginia. *Author's collection.*

to room in the eight-room house, listing items such as the eleven split-bottom chairs in Room 1 and a poplar bureau in Room 3. They also assigned a value to each. The wardrobe in Room 4 was worth $5, they said, and the clock in Room 7 was worth $1. They also went outside and among the "outdoor stuff" found a bell, wheelbarrow, spring wagon and harness. Total value of the family's property that day was $801, or nearly $25,000 today.

In another puzzling move, the commissioners also appraised some of the farm animals, a key source of revenue for the family. The Corders operated a 296-acre farm, consisting of crop land, pastures and forest.

With the appraisal, the Corders, at least the two oldest sons, were offering key parts of this operation for sale. The commissioners listed beehives, thirteen sheep and twenty-nine cows. John and Will knew that with the death of their father, they had lost his labor and guidance. Perhaps Nathan insisted on a diversified farm with animals to sell during periods of drought or times of low crop prices. Without him, however, the sons may have felt that it was time to simplify, to reduce the number of bees, sheep and especially the dairy cows, which were a seven-day-a-week obligation.[154]

It's not clear how Elizabeth felt about this strategy. It is clear, however, that three months later, in May 1892, family, friends and neighbors arrived at her home for the commissioner's sale. She watched as neighbors roamed throughout her house, inspecting the curtains and dressers. One can imagine the visitors bidding on pieces from her marriage and her life. Did the crib once hold her babies? What memories were associated with the old clock?

When it was over, twelve people had offered bids, and many of the family's possessions were gone. Dank Butler bought the trundle bed, Lizzie Turner bought a straw tick and James Yates got five beehives and a bull.

John, Will and Charles bought back some of the bees, all of the sheep and most of the cows. But Elizabeth was busier. She purchased more of the listed items than any other bidder. One can imagine her following the auctioneer, trying to retain some of the pieces. She bought carpet and curtains, a bed frame and mattress, table and chairs, a wardrobe and even four of the beehives. She was sixty-one and a widow for the second time. Presumably, these items would help her begin her life anew.

The following month, in June 1892, Elizabeth filed a document in Fauquier County Circuit Court, renouncing the terms of Nathan's will, at least the ones that applied to her. This meant that she gave up the 98 acres that Nathan had left her, or one-third of the 296-acre farm. Two months later, in August 1892, the county court appointed commissioners to assign her a specific, smaller portion of the farm, which they called her "dower." This dower was for 45 acres in two lots.[155]

They also assigned her right of way across the remainder of the farm to the main road, and they gave John and Will right of way across her land from their barnyard to a watering hole so they could water their stock. It is not clear why Elizabeth accepted a parcel of land less than half the size of her original inheritance. Perhaps the smaller piece was better land. Perhaps, although the court documents don't mention the Wheatfields mansion, the smaller parcel also included the house, thus guaranteeing her a place to live for as long as she wanted.

Indeed, three years later, in 1895, Elizabeth sold her portion of the farm to John, Will and Charles, finally giving the three boys control over the entire property. The boys paid her ninety dollars, or two dollars an acre for her forty-five acres. She retained for life the right to use one of the rooms in the house as her own, the choice of which was hers. She also insisted on "good family board" provided by John and Will at the rate of five dollars per month. This included wood for her fireplace, to be cut and stacked in her room, plus lights and washing.[156]

Elizabeth lived three more years at what was certainly a busy, if not a happy, Wheatfields. She died in 1898 at the age of sixty-seven. By then, all three boys had married, and two of them had started families. She was buried with Nathan in Rappahannock County. In her will, she bequeathed the property she owned separate from Nathan to her son, Charles, two of her grandchildren and her brother-in-law. She did not leave anything to John and Will.[157]

John was the first of the brothers to marry. In fact, he and Will married sisters, Mary Frances Cornwell and Virginia Alice. The two couples lived and farmed at Wheatfields. Will and Alice had two children; John and Mary did not have children.

John and Will and their wives sold their share of Wheatfields in 1912 and moved to Purcellville in neighboring Loudoun County. The brothers had lived and worked together their entire lives. They also died together, within days of each other, in 1915, both from stomach cancer. Will was fifty-five; John was fifty-nine. Mary Corder also died that year, at age sixty-three; Alice died in 1962, at the age of ninety-two.

Charles, the youngest of the brothers, married Lucy Nelson Priest one month after his father died. They had three children and for many years operated a store in Hume. Charles died in 1933 of hypertension. Lucy lived another twenty-three years.

After Arthur Jordan's murder, Anna, his widow, and Annie, their daughter, moved in with Anna's parents. One year later, Anna married again, this time to Robert Graves, a schoolteacher from Culpeper, Virginia. She worked as a housekeeper in Warrenton and died of consumption or tuberculosis at the age of twenty-four in 1882. Her death came two years after Arthur's death and six months after her second marriage. It's not clear what happened to Annie.

In 2018, Arthur Jordan was remembered at the National Memorial for Peace and Justice in Montgomery, Alabama. The memorial is dedicated to the thousands of Black victims of racial terror lynching in the United States. A six-foot steel box, hanging there, contains the names of Jordan and Shedrick Thompson, who was lynched on Rattlesnake Mountain, north of Warrenton, in 1932.

When the grand jury met after Arthur's death, it noted that the lynching had been done with such efficiency that no one in town was alarmed, save "the jailer and his family," an apparent reference to Colly Pattie, Horace's seventeen-year-old son, who had tried to help his father and Jordan.[158]

Colly Pattie succeeded his father as jailer after Horace died in 1885. Colly must have recalled Jordan's abduction and hanging years later when another

Top: Arthur Jordan is remembered with thousands of other lynching victims at the National Memorial for Peace and Justice in Montgomery, Alabama. *Author's collection.*

Bottom: Jordan's name and date of death are carved into a steel box that hangs at the national lynching memorial. *Author's collection.*

lynching occurred on his watch, this one involving two white men who had been convicted of murder.

In 1891, Lee Heflin and Joseph Dye were accused of killing Mrs. James Kines, a Fauquier widow, and her three children, Gilbert, four; Annie, eight; and Lizzie, ten, in a robbery attempt. The pair were convicted and sentenced to death, but their execution was delayed by the governor to allow defense attorneys to file an appeal. The delay incensed some county residents who feared the men would escape punishment.

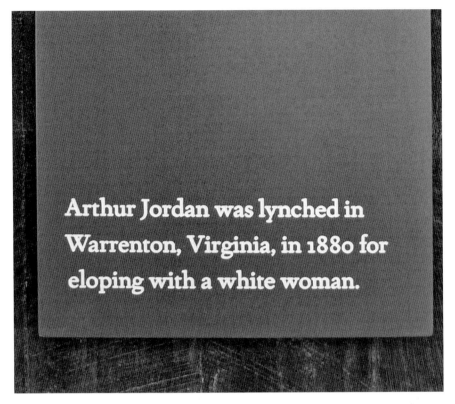

Arthur Jordan was lynched in Warrenton, Virginia, in 1880 for eloping with a white woman.

Jordan has been singled out at the memorial with a wall plaque that describes the unusual nature of his death. *Author's collection.*

Colly was aware of this anger and tried to move his prisoners to Alexandria for safekeeping. The plan was to take them by wagon to Gainesville Station to get the early morning train, according to an account by Fauquier historian John Toler. Pattie, two guards, a driver and the prisoners left Warrenton about 11:30 p.m. About an hour later, a group of about thirty-five masked men rode up to the jail and, seeing that the convicted pair was missing, headed for Gainesville.[159]

One story held that Pattie set out on the New Baltimore Road, got nearly to Buckland, seven or eight miles from Warrenton, when the mob overtook him. Pattie was about to resist when John Brawner, who was one of the men with him, told him, "Put up your pistol, Colly, or this mob will hang you, your horse and the wagon."

The masked men led Dye to a cedar tree beside the road. Heflin died on a nearby tree.

Another Warrenton resident, Joseph Arthur Jeffries, published a defense of the Heflin-Dye lynchers in words that could have been written a decade earlier in defense of the men who killed Jordan. "On the night of the day originally appointed for the execution of these men, an assembly of the best citizens from the section where the crimes were committed took the criminals from the officers of the law and quietly hanged them," he said. "If this was a crime, where lay the blame?"[160]

NOTES

Chapter 1

1. The material in chapter 1 is drawn from the *Report of Coroner's Inquisition for Arthur Jordan*, Warrenton, Virginia, January 19, 1880, Archives of the Afro-American Historical Association of Fauquier County, accessed June 1, 2022, https://aaha.pastperfectonline.com/archive/F06DF3B8-140A-419C-A4A9-384843315858.

Chapter 2

2. Martha Hodes, *White Women, Black Men: Illicit Sex in the Nineteenth-Century South* (New Haven, CT: Yale University Press, 1997), 136.
3. Joanne N. Lahey, "The Effect of Anti-Abortion Legislation on Nineteenth Century Fertility," *Demography* 51, no. 3 (June 2014): 939–48.
4. Ancestry.com. In Fauquier County, Virginia, in 1880, 148 women obtained marriage licenses as first-time brides. They ranged in age from fifteen to forty-six.
5. Arthur Meier Schlesinger, *The Rise of the City, 1878–1898* (New York: Macmillan Company, 1938), 124.
6. Peter Wallenstein, *Tell the Court I Love My Wife: Race, Marriage, and Law—An American History* (New York: Palgrave Macmillan, 2002), 61.

7. Suzanne W. Jones, *Race Mixing: Southern Fiction Since the Sixties* (Baltimore: Johns Hopkins University Press, 2004), 149.

8. Crystal N. Feimster, *Southern Horrors: Women and the Politics of Rape and Lynching* (Cambridge, MA: Harvard University Press, 2009), 9.

9. Bertram Wyatt-Brown, *Southern Honor: Ethics and Behavior in the Old South* (New York: Oxford University Press, 1982), 228.

10. Harper Lee, *To Kill a Mockingbird* (New York: Harper Perennial Modern Classics, 1960), 231.

11. *(Fredericksburg) Virginia Star*, January 10, 1880, 3.

Chapter 3

12. "Dedicated," *(Hagerstown, MD) Evening Globe*, January 5, 1880, 4A.

13. "A Negro Lynched for the Seduction of a Young White Woman," *(Memphis) Public Ledger*, January 23, 1880, 1.

14. "Virginian Vengeance," *New York Herald*, January 20, 1880.

15. "The Lynching of Arthur Jordan," *Alexandria Gazette*, January 21, 1880, 2.

16. "More Miscegenation," *Staunton Spectator*, January 6, 1880, 2.

17. William Shakespeare, *Othello* (New York: Bantam Books, 1962), Act 1, Scene 1, Line 134; Act 1, Scene 2, Line 70.

18. "Lynch Law in Virginia," *Baltimore Sun*, January 20, 1880, 1.

19. "Virginia News," *Alexandria Gazette*, January 9, 1880, 2.

20. Mattias Smångs, "Doing Violence, Making Race: Southern Violence and White Racial Group Formation," *American Journal of Sociology* 121, no. 5 (March 2016): 1,338.

21. "The Lynching of Arthur Jordan," *Alexandria Gazette*, January 21, 1880, 2.

22. "Curious Miscegenation Case from Fauquier," *Loudoun Mirror*, January 22, 1880.

23. Madeleine Forrest, "When the Rangers Came Home: Reconstructing Lives in Fauquier County, Virginia, 1865–1866" (master's thesis, Clemson University, 2012), 35.

24. Jaquilin A. Marshall, Application to President of U.S. for Special Pardon, July 25, 1865.

25. Richard L. Armstrong, *7th Virginia Cavalry* (Lynchburg, VA: H.E. Howard, 1992), 205–6.

26. *Virginia Free Press*, January 17, 1880, 2; "An Unnatural Elopement," *Winchester Times*, January 22, 1880, 3; "An Excitement at Williamsport,"

(Hagerstown) Evening Globe, January 16, 1880, 1; "Our Neighbors," *Martinsburg Independent*, January 24, 1880, 1.

27. *Virginia Free Press*, January 17, 1880, 2.

28. "Lynching of Jordan," *Gazette*, January 21, 1880, 2.

29. Interview with Ann Wisner, conducted by Shawn Nicholls, Hagerstown, Maryland, July 2019.

30. "Arrival and Arrest of the Party in Virginia," *Virginia Star*, January 21, 1880, 2.

31. Several newspapers reported on what happened to Jordan and his abductors when they stopped in Winchester, Virginia. They included "A Negro Lynched and Hung," *Staunton Spectator*, January 27, 1880, 2; "An Unnatural Elopement," *Winchester Times*, January 21, 1880, 3; "Excitement at Williamsport: A Raid into Maryland, Seizure of a Negro for Abducting a White Girl," *Virginia Star*, January 21, 1880, 2.

Chapter 4

32. "Lynched by a Mob," *Washington Post*, January 20, 1880, 1; "Lynching of Jordan," *Gazette*, January 20, 1880, 2.

33. "Lynch Law in Virginia," *Baltimore Sun*, January 20, 1880, 1; "Lynched by a Mob," *Washington Post*, January 20, 1880, 1; "Virginia Negro Lynched for a Bigamous Marriage to a White Girl," *(Minneapolis) Star Tribune*, January 21, 1880, 2; "A Shameful Outrage," *Religious Herald*, January 29, 1880, 2; "Lynch Law in Virginia," *South Branch (WV) Intelligencer*, January 23, 1880, 2.

34. 1860 U.S. Federal Census, Slave Schedule for Fauquier County, Virginia.

35. *The Will of John Corder*, Rappahannock County, Virginia, Circuit Court, Will Book B, Page 499.

36. Feimster, *Southern Horrors*, 90.

37. "Lynching of Jordan," *Gazette*, January 20, 1880, 2.

38. Ida B. Wells, *On Lynchings* (Salem: Ayer Company, 1993), 11.

39. Sheryll Cashin, *Loving: Interracial Intimacy in America and the Threat to White Supremacy* (Boston: Beacon Press, 2017), 1.

40. James McBride, *The Color of Water: A Black Man's Tribute to His White Mother* (New York: Riverhead Books, 1996), 110.

Chapter 5

41. "Lynched by a Mob," *Washington Post*, January 20, 1880, 1.
42. "Lynching of Jordan," *Gazette*, January 21, 1880, 2; "Lynching of Jordan," *Gazette*, January 20, 1880, 2.
43. Shakespeare, *Othello*, Act 1, Scene 3, Line 167.
44. Marriage license, Arthur Jordan and Anna Roe, December 26, 1878, Fauquier County Circuit Court Clerk's Office, Warrenton, Virginia.
45. James Allen, Hilton Als, Congressman John Lewis and Leon F. Litwack, *Without Sanctuary* (Santa Fe: Twin Palms Publishers, 2000), 11.
46. "Lynching of Jordan," *Gazette*, January 21, 1880, 2.

Chapter 6

47. Mrs. Robert Green to Mrs. John Jackson, 1931, Rappahannock Historical Society, Washington, Virginia.
48. 1860 U.S. Federal Census, Slave Schedule for Fauquier County, Virginia.
49. John J. Zaborney, *Slaves for Hire: Renting Enslaved Laborers in Antebellum Virginia* (Baton Rouge: Louisiana State University Press, 2012), 40.
50. Personal Property Tax Records, Fauquier County, Virginia, 1861, Fauquier County Circuit Court Clerk's Office, Warrenton, Virginia.
51. "Lynching of Jordan," *Gazette*, January 20, 1880, 2.

Chapter 7

52. *True Index*, October 2, 1880, 4.
53. Robert Beverley Herbert, *Life on a Virginia Farm* (Warrenton: Fauquier Democrat, 1968), 1.
54. *Lawrence Washington, "The Farm Diaries of Lawrence Washington, July 1885–December 1888, Waveland, Fauquier County, Virginia," George Thompson, private collection.*
55. Hugh C. Keen and Horace Mewborn, *43rd Battalion Virginia Cavalry Mosby's Command* (Lynchburg, VA: H.E. Howard, 1993), 309.
56. Forrest, *Rangers*, 3.
57. Ibid., 5.

58. John A.C. Keith, "The Home Front," in *The Years of Anguish: Fauquier County, Virginia, 1861–1865* (Warrenton, VA: Fauquier Democrat, 1965), 52; Forrest, *Rangers*, 39.

59. *News and Notes from the Fauquier Historical Society* 20, no. 1 (Spring and Summer 1998): 1.

60. James Marshall, Application to the President of U.S. for Special Pardon, May 29, 1865.

61. Personal Property Tax Records, Fauquier County, Virginia, 1861–1873, Fauquier County Circuit Court Clerk's Office, Warrenton, Virginia.

62. John K. Gott, *A History of Marshall, Fauquier County, Virginia* (Middleburg, VA: Middleburg Press, 1959), 11.

63. John K. Gott, *High in Old Virginia's Piedmont: A History of Marshall (formerly Salem), Fauquier County, Virginia* (Marshall, VA: National Bank and Trust, 1987), 53; Herbert, *Life on a Virginia Farm*, 116.

Chapter 8

64. "War on Back Creek—Seven Whites and Two Negroes Wounded," *Richmond Dispatch*, November 29, 1870, 2.

65. "Miscegenation," *Richmond Dispatch*, June 14, 1871, 2.

66. "Leaving for Parts Unknown," *Richmond Dispatch*, December 2, 1874, 2.

67. "Sent to the Penitentiary for Miscegenation," *Staunton Vindicator*, March 19, 1875, 2.

68. June Purcell Guild, *Black Laws of Virginia* (Richmond: Whittet & Shepperson, 1936), preface.

69. A. Leon Higginbotham Jr. and Barbara K. Kopytoff, "Racial Purity and Interracial Sex in the Law of Colonial and Antebellum Virginia," *Georgetown Law Journal* 77, no. 6 (August 1989): 1967–2029.

70. Johnston, *Race Relations*, 172; Smångs, "Doing Violence," 1340.

71. Francis Fedric, *Slave Life in Virginia and Kentucky*, ed. C.L. Innes (Baton Rouge: Louisiana State University Press, 2010), 16.

72. Cashin, *Loving*, 5.

73. Ibid., 3.

74. Peter Wallenstein, *Blue Laws and Black Codes: Conflict, Courts and Change in Twentieth-Century Virginia* (Charlottesville: University of Virginia Press, 2004), 14.

75. Hodes, *White Women*, 3.

76. Feimster, *Southern Horrors*, 62.

77. Ibid., 148.

78. James Kinney, *Amalgamation! Race, Sex, and Rhetoric in the Nineteenth Century American Novel* (Westport, CT: Greenwood Press, 1985), 15.

79. Wallenstein, *Tell the Court I Love My Wife*, 153.

Chapter 9

80. "An Excitement at Williamsport," *(Hagerstown) Evening Globe*, January 16, 1880, 1.

81. "Lynching of Jordan," *Gazette*, January 21, 1880, 2.

82. "An Unnatural Elopement," *Winchester Times*, January 21, 1880, 3.

83. National Association for the Advancement of Colored People, *Thirty Years of Lynching in the United States 1889–1918* (New York: NAACP, 1919), 11; W.E.B. Du Bois, "Opinion," *Crisis* 18, no. 1 (May 1919): 14; Smångs, "Doing Violence," 1,329–74, 1330; Equal Justice Initiative, *Lynching in America: Confronting the Legacy of Racial Terror*, 3rd ed. (Montgomery, AL: Equal Justice Initiative, 2015), 4.

84. Jacqueline Jones Royster, ed., *Southern Horrors and Other Writings: The Anti-Lynching Campaign of Ida B. Wells, 1892–1900* (New York: Bedford Books, 1997), 52.

85. Racial Terror: Lynching in Virginia, accessed May 12, 2022, https://sites.lib.jmu.edu/valynchings/.

86. Litwack, *Without Sanctuary*, 13.

87. Royster, *Southern Horrors*, 32.

88. Stephen V. Ash, *The Black Experience in the Civil War South* (Santa Barbara, CA: Praeger, 2010), 24.

89. Racial Terror: Lynching in Virginia, accessed June 13, 2022, https://sites.lib.jmu.edu/valynchings/

90. "Horrible Outrage in Amherst: A Negro Fiend Lynched," *Staunton Spectator*, January 13, 1880, 2.

91. Equal Justice Initiative, *Lynching in America*, 40.

92. Racial Terror: Lynching in Virginia, accessed June 13, 2022, https://sites.lib.jmu.edu/valynchings/.

93. Feimster, *Southern Horrors*, 182.

94. Racial Terror: Lynching in Virginia, accessed June 13, 2022, https://sites.lib.jmu.edu/valynchings/; Stewart E. Tolnay and E.M. Beck, *A Festival of Violence: An Analysis of Southern Lynchings, 1882–1930* (Urbana: University of Illinois Press, 1995), 50.

95. NAACP, *Thirty Years of Lynching*, 9; Edward L. Ayers, *The Promise of the New South: Life After Reconstruction* (New York: Oxford University Press, 1992), 158.

96. "Lynch Law in Virginia: A Colored Miscegenist Hung-Particulars of the Affair," *Baltimore Sun*, January 20, 1880, 1; "Lynching a Negro for a Social Indiscretion," *St. Louis Post-Dispatch*, January 22, 1880, 2.

Chapter 10

97. Michael J. Pfeifer, *Rough Justice* (Urbana: University of Illinois Press, 2004), 66; Walter White, "I Investigate Lynchings," *American Mercury*, January 1929, 77.

98. "A Vindication of the People of Warrenton," *Richmond Dispatch*, January 21, 1880, 2.

99. *Coroner's Inquisition*, Warrenton, Virginia, January 19, 1880.

100. James E. Hall, Black and White: A Historical Examination of Lynching Coverage and Editorial Impact in Select Virginia Newspapers (master's thesis, Virginia Commonwealth University, December 2001), 38.

101. Commission on Interracial Cooperation, *The Mob Still Rides: A Review of the Lynching Record, 1931–1935* (Atlanta: Commission on Interracial Cooperation, 1936), 12.

102. Wells, *On Lynchings*, 21.

103. Pfeifer, *Rough Justice*, 67.

104. Smångs, "Doing Violence," 1338.

105. Wyatt-Brown, *Southern Honor*, 458.

Chapter 11

106. Dr. Gustavus R.B. Horner, *Papers of Horner and Horner Family*, Albert and Shirley Small Special Collections Library, University of Virginia, MSS 379, Box I, Diary 10 (1876–1880), 202–4.

107. *The Most of Special Collections*, Albert and Shirley Small Special Collections Library, University of Virginia Library, accessed August 2022, https://explore.lib.virginia.edu/exhibits/show/most/walk/fright.

108. Frederick Horner, *The History of the Blair, Banister, and Braxton Families* (Philadelphia: J.B. Lippincott Company, 1897), 248.

109. *Coroner's Inquisition*, Warrenton, Virginia, January 19, 1880.

110. "Lynching of Jordan," *Gazette*, January 21, 1880, 2.

111. *Coroner's Inquisition*, Warrenton, Virginia, January 19, 1880.
112. Minutes of the Fauquier County Board of Supervisors, Warrenton, Virginia, February 20, 1880.
113. Records of the Fauquier History Museum at the Old Jail, Warrenton, Virginia, 1880.
114. "Lynching of Jordan," *Gazette*, February 3, 1880, 2
115. Robert L. Zangrando, *The NAACP Crusade Against Lynching, 1909–1950* (Philadelphia: Temple University Press 1980), 8.
116. Commission on Interracial Cooperation, *Mob Still Rides*, 11.
117. "Lynching of Jordan," *Gazette*, January 20, 1880, 2.

Chapter 12

118. "Lynched," *(Hagerstown) Evening Globe*, January 21, 1880, 2.
119. "Lynching a Seducer," *National Police Gazette*, February 7, 1880, 3; "Virginia Vengeance: Lynching a Negro for Social Indiscretion," *St. Louis Post-Dispatch*, January 22, 1880, 2; "Lynch Law," *Norfolk Virginian*, January 30, 1880, 2.
120. "Jordan Jerked," *Cincinnati Daily Star*, January 20, 1880, 1; "Served Him Right," *(Jackson, MS) Daily Clarion*, January 20, 1880, 1; *Brenham (TX) Weekly Banner*, January, 23, 1880, 2.
121. Amateur, "A Vindication of the People of Warrenton," *Richmond Dispatch*, January 21, 1980, 3.
122. Jessie Daniel Ames, *The Changing Character of Lynching* (Atlanta: Commission on Interracial Cooperation, 1942), 52.
123. "Lynching of Jordan," *Gazette*, January 20, 1880, 2.
124. Feimster, *Southern Horrors*, 37.
125. *People's Advocate*, January 24, 1880, 2.
126. "Lynched by a Mob," *Washington Post*, January 20, 1880, 1; "Lynching Seducer," *Police Gazette*, 35.
127. Ames, *Changing Character of Lynching*, 58.
128. *People's Advocate*, January 24, 1880, 2.
129. "The Virginia Outrage," *Lebanon (PA) Daily News*, January 23, 1880, 4; *Harrisburg (PA) Daily Independent*, January 27, 1880, 2.
130. "A Shameful Outrage," *Religious Herald*, January 29, 1880, 2.
131. Ames, *Changing Character of Lynching*, 51.
132. "Lynch Law," *Weekly Louisianian*, March 20, 1880, 1.
133. *Alexandria Gazette*, January 20, 1880, 2.

134. Paula J. Giddings, *Ida: A Sword Among Lions* (New York: Amistad, 2008), 153.

Chapter 13

135. "Recent Lynchings," *Richmond Daily Dispatch*, January 22, 1880, 2.
136. "The Fauquier Lynching," *Winchester Times*, January 28, 1880, 3.
137. Eric Foner, *Freedom's Lawmakers: A Directory of Black Officeholders During Reconstruction* (New York: Oxford University Press, 1993), 166.
138. "R.G.L. Paige (1846–1904)," *Encyclopedia Virginia*, accessed May 30, 2022, https://encyclopediavirginia.org/entries/paige-r-g-l-1846-1904/.
139. *News and Notes from the Fauquier Historical Society* 20, no. 1 (Spring/Summer, 1998): 1.
140. Kenneth L. Stiles, *4th Virginia Cavalry* (Lynchburg, VA: H.E. Howard, 1985), 130; William H. Fitzhugh Payne, Request of President of U.S. for Special Pardon, July 8, 1865.
141. "Fauquier Lynching," *Winchester Times*, January 28, 1880, 3.
142. *Harrisburg (PA) Daily Independent*, January 27, 1880, 2.
143. "The Virginia Outrage," *Wilmington (DE) Daily Gazette*, January 21, 1880, 4.
144. William H. Fitzhugh Payne, Request of President of U.S. for Special Pardon, July 8, 1865.
145. John Coski, "Forgotten Warrior," *North & South* 2, no. 7 (September 1999): 76.

Chapter 14

146. Interview with Darryl and Arlene Jenkins, conducted by Jim Hall and Shawn Nicholls, Fauquier County, Virginia, February 2020.
147. U.S. Census Bureau, Tenth Census, Fauquier County, Virginia, 1880.
148. "Inquisition on the Unknown Child Found at the Second Pier of the Harper's Ferry Bridge," Washington County, Maryland, Coroner's Office, October 11, 1881.
149. "Inquisition on the Death of Susan Shriver," Washington County, Maryland, Coroner's Office, June 27, 1881.
150. "Inquisition on the Case of the Infant Child of Elizabeth Ridenour," Washington County, Maryland, Coroner's Office, January 29, 1886.

151. Charles Dickens, *David Copperfield*, Jack Pulman, screenplay, 20th Century Fox Television, March 15, 1970.
152. William Shakespeare, *Romeo and Juliet* (New York: Simon & Schuster, 1992), Act 3, Scene 5, Line 206.
153. Will of Nathan Corder, Fauquier County, Virginia, Circuit Court Clerk's Office, Warrenton, Virginia, Will Book 40, page 250.

Chapter 15

154. Nathan Corder Appraisement, Fauquier County, Virginia, Circuit Court Clerk's Office, Warrenton, Virginia, Will Book 40, page 269.
155. Elizabeth Corder Renunciation, Fauquier County, Virginia, Circuit Court Clerk's Office, Warrenton, Virginia, Will Book 40, page 373; Elizabeth Corder Allotment of Dower, Fauquier County, Virginia, Circuit Court Clerk's Office, Warrenton, Virginia, Deed Book 83, page 306.
156. Deed of Elizabeth Corder, Fauquier County, Virginia, Circuit Court Clerk's Office, Warrenton, Virginia, Deed Book 86, page 216.
157. Will of Elizabeth Corder, Fauquier County, Virginia, Circuit Court Clerk's Office, Warrenton, Virginia, Will Book 42, page 321.
158. "Lynching of Jordan," *Gazette*, February 3, 1880, 2.
159. John Toler, "A Family Murdered, A Crime Avenged," *Fauquier Times*, April 24, 2019, 21.
160. Joseph Arthur Jeffries, *Joseph Arthur Jeffries' Fauquier County, Virginia, 1840–1919*, ed. Helen Jeffries Klitch, 185.

BIBLIOGRAPHY

Articles

Coski, John. "Forgotten Warrior." *North & South* 2, no. 7 (September 1999): 76.

Du Bois, W.E.B. "Opinion." *Crisis* 18, no. 1 (May 1919): 13–14.

Forrest, Madeleine. "When the Rangers Came Home: Reconstructing Lives in Fauquier County, Virginia, 1865–1866." Master's thesis, Clemson University, 2012.

Hall, James E. "Black and White: A Historical Examination of Lynching Coverage and Editorial Impact in Select Virginia Newspapers." Master's thesis, Virginia Commonwealth University, 2001.

Higginbotham, A. Leon, Jr., and Barbara K. Kopytoff. "Racial Purity and Interracial Sex in the Law of Colonial and Antebellum Virginia." *Georgetown Law Journal* 77, no. 6 (August 1989): 1967–2029.

Hodes, Martha. "Illicit Sex Across the Color Line: White Women and Black Men in the Civil War South." *Critical Matrix* 5, no. 1 (December 31, 1989): 29.

Lahey, Joanna N. "The Effect of Anti-Abortion Legislation on Nineteenth Century Fertility." *Demography* 51, no. 3 (June 2014): 939–48.

Schick, Kurt. "Slavery in Fauquier County." *News and Notes from the Fauquier Historical Society* 5, no. 4 (Fall 1983): 1–5.

Smångs, Mattias. "Doing Violence, Making Race: Southern Lynching and White Racial Group Formation." *AJS* 121, no. 5 (March 2016): 1329–74.

Wadlington, Walter. "The Loving Case: Virginia's Anti-Miscegenation Statute in Historical Perspective." *Virginia Law Review* 52, no. 7 (November 1966): 1189–223.

White, Walter. "I Investigate Lynchings." *American Mercury* 16, no. 6 (January 1929): 77–84.

Books

Alexander, Ann Field. *Race Man: The Rise and Fall of the "Fighting Editor," John Mitchell Jr.* Charlottesville: University of Virginia Press, 2002.

Allen, James, Hilton Als, Congressman John Lewis and Leon F. Litwack. *Without Sanctuary: Lynching Photography in America*. Santa Fe, NM: Twin Palms Publishers, 2000.

Ames, Jesse Daniel. *The Changing Character of Lynching: Review of Lynching, 1931–1941*. Atlanta: Commission on Interracial Cooperation, 1942.

Armstrong, Richard L. *7th Virginia Cavalry*. Lynchburg, VA: H.E. Howard, 1992.

Ash, Stephen V. *The Black Experience in the Civil War South*. Santa Barbara, CA: Praeger, 2010.

Ayers, Edward L. *The Promise of the New South: Life After Reconstruction*. New York: Oxford University Press, 1992.

Brown, Kathi Ann, Walter Nicklin and John T. Toler. *250 Years in Fauquier County: A Virginia Story*. Fairfax, VA: GMU Press, 2008.

Buck, D.A. *Fauquier County, Virginia: Birth Registry, 1853–1896*. Self-published, 1996.

———. *Fauquier County, Virginia: Death Registry, 1853–1896*. Dee Ann Buck, 1999.

———. *Fauquier County, Virginia: Marriages, 1854–1880*. Dee Ann Buck, 1996.

Cashin, Sheryll. *Loving: Interracial Intimacy in America and the Threat to White Supremacy*. Boston: Beacon Press, 2017.

Commission on Interracial Cooperation. *The Mob Still Rides: A Review of the Lynching Record, 1931–1935*. Atlanta: Commission on Interracial Cooperation, 1936.

DeRamus, Betty. *Forbidden Fruit: Love Stories from the Underground Railroad*. New York: Atria Books, 2005.

Duncan, Patricia B. *Fauquier County, Virginia: Birth Register, 1853–1880*. Westminster, MD: Heritage Books, 2008.

———. *Fauquier County, Virginia: Death Register, 1853–1896*. Westminster, MD: Heritage Books, 2012.

———. *Fauquier County, Virginia: Marriage Register, 1854–1882*. Westminster, MD: Heritage Books, 2008.

Equal Justice Initiative. *Lynching in America: Confronting the Legacy of Racial Terror*. 3ʳᵈ ed. Montgomery, AL: Equal Justice Initiative, 2015.

Fedric, Francis. *Slave Life in Virginia and Kentucky*. Edited by C.L. Innes. Baton Rouge: Louisiana State University Press, 2010.

Feimster, Crystal N. *Southern Horrors: Women and the Politics of Rape and Lynching*. Cambridge, MA: Harvard University Press, 2009.

Foner, Eric. *Freedom's Lawmakers: A Directory of Black Officeholders During Reconstruction*. New York: Oxford University Press, 1993.

Giddings, Paula J. *Ida: A Sword Among Lions*. New York: Amistad, 2008.

Gott, John K. *High in Old Virginia's Piedmont: A History of Marshall, Fauquier County, Virginia*. Marshall, VA: Marshall National Bank and Trust, 1987.

——. *A History of Marshall, Fauquier County, Virginia*. Middleburg, VA: Middleburg Press, 1959.

Groome, H.C. *Fauquier During the Proprietorship*. Baltimore: Clearfield Company, 1989.

Guild, June Purcell. *Black Laws of Virginia*. Richmond, VA: Whittet & Shepperson, 1936.

Herbert, Robert Beverley. *Life on a Virginia Farm: Stories and Recollections of Fauquier County*. Warrenton, VA: Fauquier Democrat, 1968.

Hodes, Martha. "Wartime Dialogues on Illicit Sex: White Women and Black Men." In *Divided Houses: Gender and the Civil War*, edited by Catherine Clinton and Nina Silber, 230–42. New York: Oxford University Press, 1992.

——. *White Women, Black Men: Illicit Sex in the Nineteenth-Century South*. New Haven, CT: Yale University Press, 1997.

Horner, Frederick. *The History of the Blair, Banister, and Braxton Families*. Philadelphia: J.B. Lippincott Company, 1897.

Jackson, Luther Porter. *Free Negro Labor and Property Holding in Virginia, 1830–1860*. New York: D. Appleton-Century Company, 1942.

Jeffries, Joseph Arthur. *Joseph Arthur Jeffries' Fauquier County, Virginia, 1840–1919*. Edited by Helen Jeffries Klitch. San Antonio, TX: Helen Jeffries Klitch,

Johnston, James Hugo. *Race Relations in Virginia & Miscegenation in the South, 1776–1860*. Amherst: University of Massachusetts Press, 1970.

Jones, Suzanne W. *Race Mixing: Southern Fiction Since the Sixties*. Baltimore: Johns Hopkins University Press, 2004.

Keen, Hugh C., and Horace Mewborn. *43ʳᵈ Battalion Virginia Cavalry Mosby's Command*. Lynchburg, VA: H.E. Howard, 1993.

Keith, John A.C. "The Home Front." In *The Years of Anguish: Fauquier County, Virginia, 1861-1865*, edited by Emily G. Ramey and John K.

Gott, 52–53. Warrenton, VA: Fauquier County Civil War Centennial Commission, 1965.

Kinney, James. *Amalgamation! Race, Sex, and Rhetoric in the Nineteenth-Century American Novel*. Westport, CT: Greenwood Press, 1985.

Lee, Harper. *To Kill a Mockingbird*. New York: HarperCollins Publishers, 1960.

McBride, James. *The Color of Water: A Black Man's Tribute to His White Mother*. New York: Riverhead Books, 1996.

Moran, Rachel F. *Interracial Intimacy: The Regulation of Race and Romance*. Chicago: University of Chicago Press, 2001.

National Association for the Advancement of Colored People. *Thirty Years of Lynching in the United States, 1889–1918*. New York: Arno Press, 1969.

O'Neill, Francis P. *Index of Obituaries and Marriages in the (Baltimore) Sun, 1881–1885*. Westminster, MD: Heritage Books, 2007.

Peters, Joan W. *Abstracts of Fauquier County, Virginia: Birth Records, 1853–1896*. Self-published, 1989.

Pfeifer, Michael J. *Rough Justice: Lynching and American Society, 1874–1947*. Urbana: University of Illinois Press, 2004.

Reid, Frances H. *Inside Loudoun: The Way It Was*. Leesburg, VA: Potomac Press, 1986.

Royster, Jacqueline Jones, ed. *Southern Horrors and Other Writings: The Anti-Lynching Campaign of Ida B. Wells, 1892–1900*. New York: Bedford Books, 1997.

Rushdy, Ashraf H.A. *The End of American Lynching*. New Brunswick, NJ: Rutgers University Press, 2012.

Schlesinger, Arthur Meier. *The Rise of the City, 1878–1898*. New York: The Macmillan Company, 1938.

Shakespeare, William. *The Merchant of Venice*. New York: Simon & Schuster, 1992.

———. *Othello*. New York: Bantam Books, 1962.

———. *Romeo and Juliet*. New York: Simon & Schuster, 1992.

Solinger, Rickie. *Wake Up Little Susie*. New York: Routledge, 2000.

Stiles, Kenneth L. *4th Virginia Cavalry*. Lynchburg, VA: H.E. Howard, 1985.

Taylor, Altrutheus Ambush. *The Negro in the Reconstruction of Virginia*. Washington, D.C.: Association for the Study of Negro Life and History, 1926.

Tolnay, Stewart E., and E.M. Beck. *A Festival of Violence: An Analysis of Southern Lynchings, 1882–1930*. Urbana: University of Illinois Press, 1995.

Wallenstein, Peter. *Blue Laws and Black Codes: Conflict, Courts, and Change in Twentieth-Century Virginia*. Charlottesville: University of Virginia Press, 2004.

———. *Race, Sex, and the Freedom to Marry*. Lawrence: University Press of Kansas, 2014.

————. *Tell the Court I Love My Wife: Race, Marriage, and Law—An American History.* New York: Palgrave Macmillan, 2002.

Warman, Joanne Browning, ed. *The Memorial Wall: To Name the Fallen, Warrenton, Virginia, Cemetery.* Warrenton, VA: To Name the Fallen Committee, 1998.

Washington, Lawrence. "The Farm Diaries of Lawrence Washington, July 1885–December 1888, Waveland, Fauquier County, Virginia." George Thompson, private collection.

Wells, Ida B. *On Lynchings.* Salem, NH: Ayer Company Publishers Inc., 1993.

————. *Southern Horrors and Other Writings: The Anti-Lynching Campaign of Ida B. Wells, 1892–1900.* Edited by Jacqueline Jones Royster. Boston: Bedford Books, 1997.

Wyatt-Brown, Bertram. *Southern Honor: Ethics and Behavior in the Old South.* New York: Oxford University Press, 1982.

Zaborney, John J. *Slaves for Hire: Renting Enslaved Laborers in Antebellum Virginia.* Baton Rouge: Louisiana State University Press, 2012.

Zangrando, Robert L. *The NAACP Crusade Against Lynching, 1909–1950.* Philadelphia: Temple University Press, 1980.

Government Documents

Application to the President of U.S. for Special Pardon. James Marshall. Fauquier County, Virginia. August 16, 1865.

Application to the President of U.S. for Special Pardon. Jaquilin Marshall. Fauquier County, Virginia. August 5, 1865.

Application to the President of U.S. for Special Pardon. William H. Payne. Fauquier County, Virginia. July 8, 1865.

Appraisement of the Estate of Nathan Corder. Fauquier County Circuit Court Clerk's Office. Warrenton, Virginia. February 22, 1892. Will Book 40, page 269.

Certificate of Death for Charles H. Corder. Fauquier County, Virginia. December 3, 1933.

Certificate of Death for John M. Corder. Loudoun County, Virginia. March 16, 1915.

Certificate of Death for William G. Corder. Loudoun County, Virginia. February 28, 1915.

Coroner's Inquest in the Case of Susan Shriver. Washington County, Maryland. June 29, 1881.

Coroner's Inquest in the Case of the Infant Child of Elizabeth Ridenour. Washington County, Maryland. January 29, 1886.

Coroner's Inquest in the Case of the Unknown Child Found at the Second Pier of the Harper's Ferry Bridge. Washington County, Maryland. May 25, 1881.

An Inquisition into the Death of Arthur Jordan. Fauquier County, Virginia. January 20, 1880.

Last Will and Testament of Elizabeth Corder, Fauquier County Circuit Court Clerk's Office. Warrenton, Virginia. December 28, 1895. Will Book 42, page 321.

Last Will and Testament of Nathan Corder, Fauquier County Circuit Court Clerk's Office. Warrenton, Virginia. February 22, 1892. Will Book 40, page 250.

List of Taxable Persons, Property, etc. Fauquier County, Virginia. 1856–1881.

List of Taxable Persons, Property, etc. Free Negroes and Ages. Fauquier County, Virginia. 1856–1859.

Sale List of the Estate of Nathan Corder, Fauquier County Circuit Court Clerk's Office. Warrenton, Virginia. May 24, 1892. Will Book 40, page 293.

United States Census Bureau. Census of Agriculture. Fauquier County, Virginia. 1880.

United States Census Bureau. Pauper and Indigent Inhabitants in Institutions, Poor-Houses or Asylums, or Boarded at Public Expense in Private Houses. Fauquier County, Virginia. 1880.

United States Census Bureau. Slave Schedule. Fauquier County, Virginia. 1860.

United States Department of the Interior, National Park Service. National Register of Historic Places Registration Form. Carters Run Historic District. March 27, 2014.

United States Department of the Interior, National Park Service. National Register of Historic Places Registration Form. Hume Historic District. January 9, 2008.

United States Department of the Interior, National Park Service. National Register of Historic Places Registration Form. John Marshall's Leeds Manor Rural Historic District. September 5, 2007.

United States Department of the Interior, National Park Service. National Register of Historic Places Registration Form. Markham Historic District. August 29, 2005.

United States Department of the Interior, National Park Service. National Register of Historic Places Registration Form. Old Fauquier County Jail. February 15, 1977.

United States Department of the Interior, National Park Service. National Register of Historic Places Registration Form. Orlean Historic District. June 25, 2009.

United States Department of the Interior, National Park Service. National Register of Historic Places Registration Form. Williamsport Historic District. September 7, 2001.

INDEX

T

Taylor Hotel 40
Taylor, William 40
Thomas, Lord Fairfax 55
Thompson, Shedrick 13, 18, 117

W

Ward, Dr. John 88
Warrenton 9, 19, 33, 40, 42, 43,
        49, 51, 54, 60, 68, 73, 74, 81,
        85, 92, 104, 105, 112, 117
Warrenton Cemetery 9, 11, 60, 81,
        99
Waterloo Turnpike 19, 77, 80
Wheatfields 26, 58, 114, 116
Williamsport 30, 34, 35, 37, 38, 41,
        68, 108, 109
Winchester, Virginia 37, 41, 51,
        68, 75

ABOUT THE AUTHOR

 im Hall is an award-winning journalist and popular speaker on Virginia lynchings. His book *The Last Lynching in Northern Virginia: Seeking Truth at Rattlesnake Mountain* was published by The History Press in 2016. He has a master's degree from Virginia Commonwealth University and is a former adjunct instructor at the University of Mary Washington. A native of Virginia, he is retired and lives in Fredericksburg.

Visit us at
www.historypress.com